TALES OF SPIRIT RISING
AND
SOMETIMES FALLING

Books by Arthur Waskow

Dancing in God's Earthquake
Torah of the Earth: Exploring 4,000 Years of Ecology in Jewish Thought
Seasons of Our Joy
The Bush Is Burning
The Debate over Thermonuclear Strategy
Down-to-Earth Judaism: Food, Money, Sex, and the Rest of Life
The Freedom Seder
From Race Riot to Sit-in, 1919 and the 1960s
Godwrestling
Godwrestling-Round 2

With Phyllis Ocean Berman
Freedom Journeys
Tales of Tikkun
A Time for Every Purpose Under Heaven

As co-author or co-editor
The Limits of Defense
America in Hiding: The Fallout Shelter Mania
The Tent of Abraham
Trees, Earth, and Torah: A Tu b'Shvat Anthology
Becoming Brothers
Before There Was a Before
Trees, Earth, and Torah: A Tu b'Shvat Anthology

TALES OF SPIRIT RISING AND SOMETIMES FALLING

AN ACTIVIST LIFE

RABBI ARTHUR OCEAN WASKOW

MONKFISH
BOOK PUBLISHING COMPANY
RHINEBECK, NEW YORK

Tales of Spirit Rising and Sometimes Falling: An Activist Life © Copyright 2026 by Arthur Ocean Waskow

All rights reserved. No part of this book may be used or reproduced in any manner without the consent of the publisher, except in critical articles or reviews. Contact the publisher for information.

Paperback ISBN 9781966608172
eBook ISBN 9781966608189

Library of Congress Cataloging-in-Publication Data

Names: Waskow, Arthur Ocean, 1933-2025 author
Title: Tales of spirit rising and sometimes falling : an activist life / Rabbi Arthur Ocean Waskow.
Description: Rhinebeck, New York : Monkfish Book Publishing Company, [2026]
Identifiers: LCCN 2025032796 (print) | LCCN 2025032797 (ebook) | ISBN 9781966608172 paperback | ISBN 9781966608189 ebook
Subjects: LCSH: Waskow, Arthur Ocean, 1933- | Rabbis--United States--Biography | Political activists--United States--Biography | LCGFT: Autobiographies
Classification: LCC BM755.W339 A3 2026 (print) | LCC BM755.W339 (ebook)
LC record available at https://lccn.loc.gov/2025032796
LC ebook record available at https://lccn.loc.gov/2025032797

Book and cover design by Colin Rolfe

Monkfish Book Publishing Company
22 East Market Street, Suite 304
Rhinebeck, New York 12572
(845) 876-4861
monkfishpublishing.com

This book is devoted to
Phyllis Ocean Berman
Who convinced me to write it,
Who is my beloved life-partner,
And my favorite rabbi-who-listens

I said to her:
"I will miss you."
She said to me:
"You cannot miss me.
I am in you, and
You are in me."
I said to her: "You are the key to my life."

Contents

Introduction to and from Gloria Steinem in 1968   ix

1. Growing into Me   1
2. From Closed Door to Open World   6
3. Beyond Us and Them   11
4. Learning and Teaching   18
5. Spirit and Person   23
6. Challenging Power   30
7. Institute for Policy Studies   55
8. 1968: The Longest Year   79
9. The Freedom Seder   92
10. Fabrangen   106
11. Beyond God and Torah   117
12. Reconstructionist Rabbinical College   133
13. The Shalom Center and Becoming ALEPH   146
14. Sages of All Ages   161
15. God and Earth   167
16. Ishmael and Isaac   178
17. Bashert   191
18. Illness, Death, and Grief   196
19. The Ultimate Crisis in Jewish Values   208

Afterword by Rabbi Phyllis Ocean Berman   219

Introduction to and from Gloria Steinem in 1968

It was a week day, a workday, in 2012. I was sitting at my computer, writing someone a letter. My phone rang. It rang again a few minutes later, and four or five times after that.

The calls all started the same way: "Were you watching Oprah?"—"Ummm. No. Why do you ask?"

So they told me: Oprah had been interviewing Gloria Steinem and to close the interview asked her whether she remembered any life-changing moments she had lived through. Steinem answered that someone she hadn't known named Arthur Waskow had made a lasting impression on her work.

She was at the Chicago Democratic Convention in 1968. "I was distributing leaflets for the California farm workers and somebody sneered at me, 'You're not a farm worker!'" She said it wasn't just the one sneer. She was overwhelmed with the protests, the violence. She was frustrated and baffled by what seemed the uselessness of her work. "So in this moment of despair I turned to somebody I did not know—it turned out to be Arthur Waskow—and said I would quit—it was all useless anyway. But he said something like, 'Keep on going, what you are doing really matters!'" She hadn't seen Waskow since and she was hoping that he would hear this. And she spoke of the profound effect that that brief moment had in empowering her to go on with her work on behalf of all women—and, therefore, on behalf of us all.

Next day there were three emails. They told more or less the same story. And one of them ended—"I know that in that moment you were just doing what you do—calling each of us to be the best they can be. I thought you would be heartened to know that such small moments do ripple forth to energize the wonderfully interconnected whole."

In the summer of 1968 neither Gloria nor I had the language of Spirit. So why am I putting this story of the Spirit rising at the beginning of this book? Because by 2012 I had learned that language. Indeed, I was struck in 2012 and still today by the two levels of meaning in the story. First level: *"You never know!"* You never know what words, what acts, can reshape a life or destroy it with despair. Second level: You can know that Spirit does know. It knows Love. But you never know when the Spirit will rise, or sometimes fall.

I didn't know how to reach Gloria Steinem, but I knew how to reach her close friend and colleague, co-founder of *Ms. Magazine*, Letty Cottin Pogrebin. I called Letty to tell her the story, and asked her to ask Gloria to call me.

Fifteen minutes later my phone rang—Gloria. We agreed to meet at her home in New York. There we had an exhilarating conversation not about the past but about the future. We planned a fruitful collaboration in which, suddenly, there was a new moment of the Spirit rising. That story is later in this book.

This book is about what I have learned when I think or feel the Spirit rising, falling, disappearing in relation to a particular moment—a problem, an insight, an incident. But a tale that affected me most deeply might not be the moment in others' lives that for them was most important, delightful, or demoralizing. Or they may have learned something different from living in the same story.

So some people whose wisdom I have learned may say that I misunderstood what they intended. Or maybe that I ignored what for them was the true meaning. I send blessings to all my teachers, to all who lived with me in these tales. It is only my own feelings that I can honestly report. I ask their and your forgiveness for any misunderstandings.

Long ago when I was learning to become a historian, I was taught there was no such person as a "neutral" historian. The best we could do was to name our biases, and let our readers take account of them. So I can do that quickly: I seek to celebrate the Breath of life that intertwines all life, at least on Planet Earth. My guide toward doing that is all the richness of Torah, spoken and written and reinterpreted for at least three thousand years. I understand this Torah as a continuing family report, with much in it that is glorious and generous and much that is dangerous. I seek to encourage the urge to express and work for love, justice, truth, and Shalom that impels many human beings. I try to understand and calm the urge toward power-over, selfishness, and greed that impels many human beings. I seek to stand with the dispossessed and disempowered. I aim to speak truth to the disempowered—more urgent than speaking truth to power. I aim to take a reasonable place in an inclusive eco-democracy, where different identities among us—human and other-than-human—try hard to serve each other's needs.

That is me as I write. It comes from nearing the end of my struggles. It is something like an ethical will; perhaps it belongs at the end of the book.

I
Growing into Me

I remember a series of moments, all happening in various stages of growing into my self, and then retreating as the Spirit fell. All happening in some version of "school."

In the second grade, we started to learn arithmetic. Our teacher gave us a test each Friday on what we had learned each week. After about three weeks, I realized that the questions from 1 to 10 started out easy and got harder; questions 9 and 10 were always the hardest of all. So I answered 9 and 10 and left the others blank. I had solved two tests: numbers and the deeper puzzle of the teacher's process. But the teacher was playing a different game. Week after week, my paper got returned with a failing mark: D for Deficient.

Still, I knew what I knew. I stuffed the paper in my desk and kept on proving I knew the answers to the hardest questions. Until the PTA meeting. Til my mother came to meet my teacher, who said, "He's flunking arithmetic. Otherwise, he's doing fine!"

"Flunking arithmetic!?" my mother said. "That can't be. He understands it perfectly!"

So they palavered for a while. Then they came and confiscated all the papers I had stuffed in my desk. I explained about questions 9 and 10 and they both said firmly that was not acceptable. They agreed to require that I answer all the questions, bring the tests home, get them signed by my mother, and bring them back to the teacher, signed. I surrendered.

I didn't think they were right, but what could I do? So I answered all the arithmetic questions every Friday, even the ones so simple they were silly, got the paper marked—E for Excellent—took it home for my mother to sign, and brought it back for my teacher.

They did recognize that I was a smart kid and needed something to occupy me, or maybe mollify me. So the teacher announced to me and the class that every morning I would be consulting an outdoor thermometer and humidity-measure, and announce the numbers to the class. I did this for a week and realized the information made no difference to anybody at all. I resigned. My "rebellion" turned infinitesimal.

* * *

The next time was more consequential. In the 12th grade, in 1950, I was the editor-in chief of the school paper. Most of the content was pretty boring. What was exciting was a weekly visit to the printer, still using a Linotype, which heated lead to the boiling point, made it take the form of the next letter in the story, and thus cast a line of type.

But I got hold of one story that excited me. Baltimore's school system was racially segregated, and my own school was not only all-white but all-male. In every high school was a "Future Teachers of America Club," and there was a city-wide FTA. Only there was not one "city-wide" FTA, but two. One white, one Black. I thought that was crazy. Future Teachers and the future America would still be racially segregated? So I wrote an editorial describing and denouncing.

Somebody on the staff took a copy to the faculty adviser, and he vetoed it. In a century of student journalism, that had never happened before—at least so far as anyone alive knew. So I went to the vice-principal. He seemed to be a kind and decent man. He said, "Arthur, in my life-time and in yours, there's not going to be racial desegregation in the Baltimore school system. What's the point?"

So I turned to my parents. I had a plan. A former editor of my student paper was now a reporter for the *Baltimore Sun*, a fine newspaper in that generation. I was pretty sure he would think it a good story, and so would the *Sun*. But my parents were scared. They thought Johns Hopkins University would not admit a trouble-making Jewish kid. Hopkins then had three racist policies: one Negro a year in the undergraduate school, a quota on Jewish students, and one Jew on the faculty (and he was a world-renowned European scholar). My family couldn't afford to send me to a really good college anywhere outside Baltimore, where I would have to live in a dorm. Hopkins was essential.

I surrendered again. And I didn't get to say my say for sixty-one years. That tale you can read later on page 153.

* * *

I did get into Hopkins. In my senior year I took an excellent course in the period of Reconstruction and "Redemption" in the South—the brief period of Black liberation and the restoration of white supremacy through Ku Klan Klan terrorism and Northern cooperation with it through withdrawal of the U.S. Army from the South.

The course was taught by C. Vann Woodward, a historian so eminent that his review of that history played an important role in the Supreme Court desegregation decision on May 17, 1954, close to the end of my senior year. I cried with joy and relief when I heard the radio news reports. (It came while my high-school vice-principal was still alive, hale and hearty—and so was I. And Baltimore obeyed; my school was peacefully integrated in the fall of 1954.)

Woodward assigned us a series of histories of the period, ranging from the Black sociologist W. E. B. Du Bois, to white supremacists, to puzzled and confused white "moderate" racists. For each, he encouraged us to connect the politics of the historian to the history he wrote. Then, a few weeks later, he assigned us one of his own books on Reconstruction. I read it dutifully over a weekend and was deeply impressed. His thesis was that a combination of Northern economic power and Northern greed plus American racist bias—especially intense in the South, but present everywhere—had brought about the collapse of Reconstruction.

When we came back to the seminar, I asked whether he thought he, like the other historians we had read, had been influenced by his political beliefs in coming to his historical conclusions. To my astonishment, he got angry. I thought my question seemed obvious, and figured his answer would be something like, "Sure! But I tried to recognize and guard against my bias. The best I could do was warn my readers to recognize my bias and help me guard against it." Instead, he got angry, as if I'd attacked him.

I backed off. I didn't apologize or back down, but I shut up. I needed his recommendation to some really good graduate school in U.S. history; I couldn't go to battle against him. I didn't even want to—after all, his book had convinced me! But his anger and my silence still nag at me. Almost seventy years later.

After that course ended, I asked for his recommendation and he gave it cheerfully. He told me there were two great departments of history in the country, filled with fine historians: Columbia and Wisconsin, but at Columbia, the great historians were always away—off-campus, giving speeches and what-not. At Wisconsin, they were always there, teaching, meeting students, leading seminars. His own mentor from his days in grad school was there: Howard Beale. Still, Columbia was more glamorous, and a lot closer to home. Which did I want him to write?

I said, "Wisconsin."

※ ※ ※

Most of my first year in Madison felt rocky. I joined Beale's seminar, where it was normal for first-year grad students to do a research paper or two, test their ability by combining competition and cooperation with the others. Many of us were second, third, fourth, even fifth-year. By that time, they should be working on their Ph.D. dissertations, on the verge of being faculty in a college themselves. In that first year, I felt outclassed. They all seemed to have read more than I had, thought deeper than I had.

One week, Mr. Beale had us read about President Theodore Roosevelt's urge to elevate the Unites States to be recognized as one of the great world powers. He decided to make that clear in 1908 by sending what the press called "The Great White Fleet"—that is, the cream of the U.S. Navy—to appear in major ports throughout the world. But the real target was Japan, where riots against Japanese workers in California had stirred anti-American demonstrations. Additionally, Japan had just won a naval war against Imperial Russia, and Roosevelt wanted to warn the Japanese government against testing U.S. imperial power in the Pacific.

After our seminar had discussed the emergence of U.S. overseas imperialism for a while, Beale abruptly asked, "What do you think was the response of the Japanese government?"

I raised my hand. "Pearl Harbor," I said.

Beale's face turned red. "Where did you get that?" he snapped.

"Common sense," I said. "No government that has just defeated a great power is going to like being humiliated. It took them almost forty years to get strong enough, but they took revenge."

Beale sat quiet for a moment. Then he sighed and said, "I'm sorry. I've been getting some research done in the Japanese archives, and you are exactly right. I thought somebody had somehow gotten into my notes."

From then on, even during my strange deviation from grad student into Congressional legislative assistant, Beale treated me like a knowledgeable, or at least sensible, fledgling historian. More importantly, I thought of myself that way.

2
From Closed Door to Open World

Several times in life, I have learned that what seems like a personal disaster—a door slammed in my face—can become an adventure when the door opens to a new world on the other side. The Spirit that seems to fall has actually risen. The first time was when I got swept from historical research into political activism.

A little background: While a graduate student at the University of Wisconsin, I decided in 1958 to work in the Congressional campaign of a very young lawyer (a Democrat) named Bob Kastenmeier, who lived in a tiny town called Watertown. There was no chance he would win, but I could learn a lot by working for him.

He was an unusual politician. He went into politics because as a really young second lieutenant in 1945, he was sent to Japan where he saw Hiroshima about six weeks after the bomb. He went into public life to make sure that would never happen again.

When he gave speeches, he used to keep his hands in his pockets so that nobody could see that they were trembling. Because he was so scared when he gave speeches.

In summer 1958, there were two issues of military intervention that he thought ran the risk of war. One was whether the U.S. should risk conflict against China, the real China, to protect the tiny unpopulated off-shore islands of Quemoy and Matsu that were under the control of the fake China on Taiwan. (In those days, you couldn't even say "China" about the government that ruled the biggest population in the world. It was called "Red China," and the only place you were allowed to call "China" was Taiwan.) So Kastenmeier opposed sending U.S. troops to hold those islands, and the whole Wisconsin Democratic party said, "Yeah, yeah, yeah! You're right!"

Then a nationalist movement erupted in Lebanon, and the Eisenhower Administration sent a contingent of the Marines there. Bob Kastenmeier said that was a bad idea. "The U.S. shouldn't be intervening in Lebanon," and half the Democratic party said, "Yeah, yeah, yeah! You're right!" But the other half said "No!"—especially liberal Jews of the city of Madison who were worried that Lebanese nationalism would endanger Israel. And Kastenmeier was stunned. He thought it was all the same issue: Don't send troops to police the world.

He asked me to do a research piece for him on Lebanon and America, saying, "Maybe I'm wrong. I don't know. Figure it out." So I did the first research I'd ever done on policy issues in the Middle East. I came back and said, "You were right altogether."

And then he won! There was a totally unexpected Democratic sweep in the 1958 election, and this impossible "politician" won. He went off to Washington and I went back to being a graduate student. And I started pursuing what was going to be my doctoral dissertation. In studying with Hans Gerth, a brilliant radical sociologist, I'd become interested in the sociology of riots. In studying with Howard Beale, not only a brilliant historian of the American Empire, racism and the South, and the nature of history-writing itself, a brilliant historian, I became interested in research on race relations. I put them together, to do a dissertation on a series of race riots in the summer of 1919.

In 1958-59, race riots seemed to be an antiquarian thing. There hadn't been any in America since the early 1940s, and that seemed a long time in U.S. race relations. (Little did I know that by 1965, when I finished the book that came out of the dissertation, the Watts Rebellion would be raging in Los Angeles, fulfilling my finding that police behavior almost always lit the match to racial violence.)

I was fascinated by the summer 1919 riots, and realized that I was going to have to go to Washington DC to spend a serious amount of time, because the National Archives had a lot of material on them: the army had intervened, the FBI had poked around...

So I applied for a grant from the Social Science Research Council to go to Washington and do this research. I got turned down. About three weeks later, Bob Kastenmeier and his wife Dorothy came back to visit Madison, and we had lunch. He asked what was going on in my life, and I said, "Well, I'm coming to Washington, but I don't know how I'm going to live there. I need to come—not only do I need to do research there, but my wife, Irene Elkin, has gotten a post-doctoral fellowship at the National Institute of Mental Health, so doubly I need to go. But I didn't get this grant."

He said, "Hmmm. Well, why don't you come work for me about one-fourth time? That'll pay you about as much as the grant would have paid you, you can keep on working on the dissertation, and you can write speeches or letters or whatever." So that gave my life a totally unexpected turn away from academia. I worked for him for the next year and a half, and though the Wisconsin history department was a great department, I learned a lot more about American society working in that atmosphere in the House of Representatives.

In those days, there was no bureaucracy. I was handed everything from a constituent's letter saying "Whatever happened to my Social Security check?" to "What *is* nuclear deterrence, anyway? Is it real, and if so, what should we do about it? What does it mean to deter?" All those levels of reality.

In Kastenmeier's office I met an extraordinary guy named Marc Raskin, who was working for several different members of Congress to create what we called the Liberal Project. We were examining all over again not how to "win" the Cold War but even the assumptions behind it, which nobody had done since it began.

Kastenmeier decided to look into what the Army Chemical Corps was doing, because they were trying to reverse a policy, set during World War II, that the U.S. would never be the first to use chemical or biological chemical weapons. The Chemical Corps claimed they were developing "non-lethal" weapons through research at Fort Detrick near Frederick, Maryland. Kastenmeier asked me to research what was going on there, and although it was all supposed to be top secret, these frustrated biologists were publishing their research with a barely shimmery cover on what it was, where it was, and how it was. If they had been forbidden to publish their work, they would've been exiled to Siberia in their professions. I mean, if you can't publish, who are you?

So they did in fact publish. And we dug up some amazing stuff. Several people died from their "non-lethal" research. One civilian electrician who came in to change the light bulbs died of pneumonic plague, a variant of bubonic plague. There was a universal international treaty that any occurrence whatsoever of plague must be immediately reported by the government where it occurred to the World Health Organization, to prevent a pandemic. But we discovered that this guy who had died of pneumonic plague had not been reported to the World Health Organization til four or five months after the death. It seemed extremely strange. We started poking around and demanded that the Army Chemical Corps explain how come. They sent the commandant of the Corps in full regalia—ribbons, medals, all that stuff—to the Congressman's office.

The first thing he said was that he was prepared to give a total explanation of everything involved, on condition that the Congressman accepted security clearance. Kastenmeier said, "No, that means that I can't talk about whatever it is. If you tell me it all, that it'll be totally under seal, and that's not why I was elected. I can't do that." So the general said, "Well, in that case, I can only tell you…" And what he basically said was, this death from pneumonic plague had happened while Nikita Krushchev, the head of the Soviet Union, was traveling in the United States. And the Chemical Corps—this guy—decided that it would be bad for American foreign policy if they published the fact of this, what they were working on, while Krushchev was in the country.

We said, "Well, did you consult any higher military authority?" No. "Did you consult the State Department, or any diplomatic authority?" No. "You made the decision totally on your own?" Yes.

I remember feeling my hair standing on end. I mean, it was an American treaty that they had violated. And he had violated it on his own responsibility, or so he claimed anyway. There was no question that he considered himself right and would do it again. And then he and all his stars and medals just went away.

We were just sitting there, a little stunned. I said, "Well, you gotta make a big thing out of this." And Kastenmeier said, "No." I said, "Why?" He said, "If I personalize it to the degree of focusing on this guy, they will come after me in Wisconsin with everything they've got. So I will keep focusing on the *issue*, on the issue of no first use of bio- or chemical weapons, but I'm not going to personalize it because that would step over the line, so far as they're concerned."

That was for me a measure of how far and how not far it was possible to go. I remember thinking about C. Wright Mills, who wrote a book called *The Power Elite*, about how corporations and the military really ran America, and I'd thought it was bullshit. When I was a graduate student in Wisconsin, it didn't look like that to me. The university was bubbling with liberal energy, and the state was responding. So I thought then, *This is silly*. But now I realized, there really is a power elite, and they have enough power to make even Bob Kastenmeier back off about half an inch. Not more than half an inch, but at least half an inch, he had to back off.

Twice the Spirit rose, in the very moment of falling. The discovery of how powerful the military were, and how vulnerable the elected Congressperson, shook me about American democracy. But if the Spirit cared about me, my own wisdom, the Spirit rose. And the Falling/ Rising were the same!

3

Beyond Us and Them

It's Madison, Wisconsin, 1956. I'm a graduate student, talking casually with Marsel Heisel, another grad student—a visitor from Turkey. Marcel: "One of the glorious moments of my life in Istanbul was in 1953, when we had a wonderful festival." Me: "What was it celebrating?"

"The great Turkish capture of Constantinople in 1453."

"Celebration?! That was the greatest disaster in the history of the West!"

Marsel smiles.

"Oh. The West," I say.

* * *

I spent the summer of 1969 in Israel and in visits to the Palestinian territories, then newly occupied by Israel after the 1967 war. Irene Elkin, then my wife, had close family in a Labor Zionist kibbutz in the Negev desert. That kibbutz became our home for a couple of months.

We decided to visit the traditional site in Hebron of the grave of Abraham, who is claimed as progenitor and pioneer by both the Jewish and Muslim communities. We rented a car and drove off. And as we entered the outskirts of Hebron, the car began to sputter and buck. We pulled over, confused. Neither of us knew much about automobile machinery. We stood there looking helpless.

More than baffled or helpless: we felt frightened. Here we were, two American Jews, stranded in a land we did not know, a land where no one knew where we were. A land whose people had good reason to be hostile to strangers who, so far as they knew, supported a military occupation of their country. (I knew perfectly well that even a so-called "benign" occupation rubbed hard against the feelings of those occupied.)

Two Palestinian men came over. They spoke a bare and broken English and we had no Arabic beyond "Salaam." Gesturing, they asked permission to poke around the car. We gulped and said okay.

After a few minutes one of them began to say, "Flud! Flud." We finally recognized that he was telling us the brake fluid had run out, and that's why the car was acting so peculiar.

Again with gestures and a few words, they pointed us to let them push the car off the road. Our fear grew higher—now we would be in a place even more hidden, more mysterious—but there seemed to be no alternative.

Off the road, several men who seemed to be expert car mechanics came over to work on the flud. And—amazing!—a teen-age boy came out of a house bearing an enormous copper tray. On it were two cups of coffee, and a steaming pitcher filled with more.

When I realized this was meant for us, my first thought was that there was no gas station in America that would have welcomed any customer, let alone a stranger, with a cup of coffee. At last, my heart slowed down, my fears vanished like the steam from the pitcher. And I realized that our forlorn trip to visit Father Abraham had been successful after all—even more successful than visiting his grave. In the Palestinians who welcomed us, our shared forefather Abraham, famed for hospitality, had come alive, was still alive.

Since that day, I never felt fear when meeting Palestinians. Some were no doubt dangerous—ready to attack civilians. During the rest of that summer, I met a number of leaders and officials of their occupied community in the West Bank, Gaza, and East Jerusalem. A few were hostile, but by far most shared with me their pain at living under occupation, their hope for a self-governing state of their own, at peace with Israel and Jordan, which had occupied them for decades before 1967. I came back to America convinced that we should be encouraging what people slowly began to call the two-state solution.

But for me, underneath the politics was that transformative moment when I realized that our peoples were not doomed to fear and hatred of each other. At last I knew: That was the Spirit rising.

* * *

In the spring and summer of 1968, after the death of Martin Luther King Jr., a project he had been planning was carried out by the Southern Christian Leadership Council. It was to bring thousands of low-income Americans of all "colors" and "races" together in Washington, DC in a tent city they called Resurrection City.

The hope was to expand the transformative movement to protest not just racism but the subjugation of people through poverty that could have been long ago ended by the richest society in history.

The local DC Jewish Community Council had what they called a Committee on Urban Affairs. Somebody knew I was Jewish and had written a book called *From Race Riot to Sit-in*. The first half of the book was from my dissertation about a long hot summer of race riots in 1919. So I guess the book qualified me as a Jewish expert on urban affairs, and the Committee invited me to join and bring my expertise to how the Jewish community might deal with "urban affairs"—especially Resurrection City. That seemed decent enough, maybe even valuable to do, although my Jewishness was pretty nominal in those days.

I went to a meeting of the Committee beginning at noon one day that spring. While I was in the room, the Jewish Community Council got a phone call from someone connected with Resurrection City. The caller reported that a new contingent of protestors had arrived that morning from a long bus trip from somewhere deep in the South. Their people badly wanted to take showers. They had been offered shelter at a Catholic church but there were only one or two showers in the church and they needed more. So they asked around and were told that the Jewish Community Center, which had a gym, had plenty of showers, and they called the Jewish Community Center (JCC) to ask permission to bring their people to take showers.

The JCC said no.

The urban affairs committee of the Jewish Community Council was horrified. A few people were upset about what bad publicity this might mean for the Jewish community, but most said they were upset because it was a traditional Jewish value to offer welcome and hospitality, especially to the poor. That tradition went all the way back to Abraham, who kept his tent open on all four sides for travelers to find shelter and food.

So all the *machers* (weighty Jews—well-known and respected community leaders) turned themselves to figuring out how to change the JCC answer from no to yes. Most of them—in fact all but one—started trying to call their *macher* friends, figuring they would be able to tug the board or maybe were on the board of the JCC, and could get the refusal reversed.

There were four or five of us who were new to this committee. As Jews we were marginal—not *machers*. We clustered sitting on the floor at the edge of this cloistered office. To our surprise, we were joined by someone who everyone else thought was a *macher* but who felt himself a radical. He had fought in the "Israeli War of Independence" with Palmach, a left-wing army, and had come back to the United States. He introduced himself to the four or five of us who didn't know any of these people; his name was Arnold Sternberg.

One of the marginal among us, drawing on demonstrations at Columbia University and elsewhere, suggested we go to the JCC and simply open the doors, inviting the people from Resurrection City to come take showers. Sternberg approved and said he would be glad to call his friends who were also Jewish radicals and have them come at 5pm that afternoon.

The exec of the Jewish Community Council stood there listening in horror, imagining the headlines in newspapers the next day. He broke into our conversation. He said, "I am sure we can get the board overnight to change the decision, but just in order to reach them on the phone is a real problem, and it will take us this evening and tonight to get them to change by tomorrow morning. Why do you need to set the deadline to 5pm?"

Sternberg looked at him and said, "Because the *Ma'ariv* prayer is at 5pm and I intend to *daven Ma'ariv* at the JCC."

I felt like a lightning bolt had hit. This didn't make any sense at all, and it made all the sense, all the imagination, in the entire world. I don't think Arnold Sternberg even *davened* during a normal day or night, but for him this was prayer, showers for the poor, religion as an activist transformation. I didn't even know what to call this kind of response, but it felt right. Utterly right.

Turned out, with the energy of a possible shower-in in the air, the phone calls from the *machers* worked much faster than they thought. By 5pm the JCC had stopped whistling dixie and changed their tune. So we never needed to *daven Ma'ariv* at the other JCC. The lesson sunk in to me. Or maybe I should say, the lesson and the Spirit lifted me as the Spirit rose. That moment became one of the seeds of the Freedom Seder (see below). In fact, we asked Sternberg's daughter, who was very young, to come chant the four questions at the first Freedom Seder.

* * *

One of our closest friends, Dr. Barbara (Bobbi) Breitman is a psychotherapist and a co-founder of the discipline of Jewish spiritual direction. She was born on Christmas Eve, and her mother gave her the middle name of Eve, not to praise the heroine of Eden but to mark indelibly the evening she was born.

About twelve years ago, this honoring of Christmas Eve began to move Bobbi in a way neither she nor her mother imagined. In her words, "I began imagining that night as the time when billions of human beings imagine the birth of messiah—a great tsunami of hope and comfort, all around the globe. Why not ride that wave like a surfer, even though I could plainly see that the messianic days of peace and justice were not yet here? So I called a bunch of my friends to surf the wave with me on Christmas Eve. They came! And I asked Hazzan Jack Kessler to sing the bold yet plaintive Yiddish song, 'Shnirele Perele,' which affirms that *Mashiach*—Messiah—is coming this very year."

We sang it together in Yiddish, and I wrote an English that fit the same melody:

Shnirele perele gilderne fon	Ribbons, pearls, so the story's told,
Meshiekh ben dovid zist oybn on	Mashiach ben David flies a flag of gold
halt a beckher in der rekhter hant	raises a wine-cup in his right hand
Makht a brockhe afn gantsn land	and gives his blessing upon every land.
Oi, omeyn ve-omeyn dos iz vvor	Ameyn, ameyn, this is true and clear—
Meshiekh vet kumen hayntiks yor.	Mashiach is coming this very year!

Could the Spirit resist rising to such a voice, such hope?

So every year, year after year, we join with Bobbi, with Jack, with each other, with the Spirit, to sing out what needs to happen.

* * *

For many years, Phyllis and I were members of a group of four couples (with Bahira and Shaya, Shoshana and David, Shefa and Rachmiel, three of whom shared an April 8th birthday)—"The Octet"—who took vacations together. In the early aughts we chose the west coast of Mexico. As we boarded the airliner, I muttered I was not feeling well. Phyllis asked whether I wanted to cancel, but I said no.

By the time we got to Puerto Vallarta, I was groggy. As we got off the plane to meet our friends, Shoshana said hello and got no answer from an always talkative me. She, a former nurse, looked more closely at me and then said sharply, "Do you want to die, right now?!" I managed a "No." She said, "Then you need to go to a hospital right now."

We did. The hospital decided I needed an emergency removal of my appendix, ready to explode. Taking a medical history, the surgeon asked what work I did. I said, "Rabbi." His face lit up and he said, "Me, I am Catholic. But it is all One, yes? It is all One!"

"Yes," I managed to say, through tears.

Once my belly was open, the doctors saw that my gall bladder was full of stones and decided that it too needed emergency removal. I was on the operating table for four hours. I awoke ready for a joyful vacation, grateful for the surgeons and for the Spirit rising in tune with the surgeon's rough-cut version of the Sh'ma: God is One!"

4
Learning and Teaching

Howard K. Beale, my major professor as I studied for the doctorate at Wisconsin, saw himself as a Christian pacifist, a radical historian in the tradition not of Marx but of Charles A. Beard's *Economic Interpretation of the Constitution*. His central seminar for grad students had in it many who were cutting their teeth on neo-Marxist analysis but did not see the labor movement as the crux of transformation, nor cultural and moral questions as profoundly political. Others were attached to conventional liberalism and still others to Gandhian thought.

Beale loved to pose a question of historical analysis that might test all these schools of thought. He would sit back, smiling, as his students grew in historianship by arguing with each other.

There was also another important aspect of his teaching. He realized that many of his students were not the WASP Americans who had populated most U.S. History classes in the past. Some of his colleagues were uncomfortable admitting people like me to their fellowship. As late as 1959, Beale reported that the department was arguing whether an American Jewish professor from another university could "fit in." Would he be able to take on the habits of WASP etiquette?

Sometimes Beale invited his graduate students over for dinner. One evening as we sat down to dinner, we saw a dish in the center of the table bearing a vegetable none of us had ever seen. After a pained silence, one of us—Gerd Korman, a Jewish kid whose first language was Yiddish and who turned that into a unique dissertation by studying Yiddish newspapers in Milwaukee—asked, "Mr. Beale, what is that vegetable, and how do you eat it?" "It's an artichoke!" said Beale and explained the esoterica of eating it.

Ever since then, artichokes have been for me a symbol of—not quite justice or equality, but compassion. A complex dish of privilege and compassion. Not the dish of Eden's Garden, but perhaps the best that someone steeped in privilege could reach to.

* * *

Ramparts magazine published the very first version of what became *The Freedom Seder* in February 1969, just in time for people to absorb and use as their *Haggadah* (story/telling) for Passover in April.

Years and years later, when I already knew how extraordinary a spiritual giant Reb Zalman Schachter-Shalomi was, he told me that he'd read the *Ramparts* version, and it convinced him that his vision of a new paradigm of Judaism was not a crazy dream but an achievable goal.

Why? Precisely because we didn't know each other. I wasn't a disciple of his, he was not a comrade of mine. We were creating a new paradigm, for Judaism, each out of our own experience of what seemed very different worlds, each out of our own realization of the need.

As he spread and grew his network during the seventies, he found people utterly new to him who like me were nurturing a piece of a new Judaism that belonged in the new Jewish jigsaw puzzle. Many of them were women. For them to transform male-dominant Judaism to meet their hopes and needs was an enormous task. Yet in one generation they accomplished most of it with help from the Spirit rising, swiftly flapping unused wings. They accomplished the crucial part: making invincibly clear that they were no "extra" in the new Judaism, but part of its heart—decision-making in what it would become.

The first face-to-face meeting between Reb Zalman and me came almost two years after the first Freedom Seder. I heard he would be leading a *Shabbat*-evening service at George Washington University Hillel, and I'd heard enough about him to want to be there. So I went. There were about forty students present. He looked us over, and announced, "With your permission, I would like to separate the men and women."

I called out, "No!" He looked around. Puzzled.

"What?"

When I first wrote *The Freedom Seder*, I didn't know that the rush of Spirit had many women in it; but by early 1971, I knew—with passion from my eyebrows to my toenails. I said, "You said, 'With our permission.' Not with my permission!"

"Oh!" said Zalman. "I didn't mean the old *mechitza*, separating women and telling them to be silent. I am experimenting with spiritual dynamics: Would the intensity of Spirit be greater in separate responsive bundles? How about this: We separate not bodies but voices. The men and women respond to each other in chanting. Is that okay?" I said yes, and we began the *davening*.

At the end of the evening, I had no idea whether the antiphonal chanting had lifted Spirit higher, but I knew that this teacher, steeped in millennia of learning, paid attention when a novice said no. This was a teacher I could learn from.

* * *

In 1980, the festival of Shavuot, which the Rabbis turned from celebrating the spring harvest into celebrating the revelation of Torah, I joined about thirty other people for an all-night study. We were sitting on the porch at the home of Reb Zalman. It was a big house in the Mt. Airy neighborhood of Philadelphia, and it had room for a prayer space, a couple of students of Zalman's to live on the third floor, and in the basement, an agricultural reaper and a harvester that Zalman had picked up cheaply at state agricultural fairs. He was still dreaming that *B'nai Or* (Children, or more literally, Sons of Light) would become an agricultural settlement and save *Hassidic* mystical Judaism from the dark night of the Holocaust.

So we were drinking lemonade and talking about what it could possibly have meant to receive the gifts of Torah. I said I thought that the band of runaway slaves who scurried their way out of *Mitzrayyim*, the tight and narrow space, like being caught between a rock and a hard place, was a single file line of runaways. Each runaway knew two or three people in front of them and two or three people behind them. That was all. There was no larger community.

Then they reached Sinai. The people folded back on itself. They began to schmooze, to chat with one another, a circle where you could see a companion, across the circle. They started to wonder out loud what was supposed to happen at this mountain. They became a community.

Zalman was at the center of our own small community. He listened to me talk about the change from single file to folded circle. Then he turned and spoke to two young rabbis in the crowd—one Orthodox and one Reconstructionist. He said, "Have you learned from Waskow?" They both said, "Uhh, yeah!" He pulled their arms so they were standing right beside him, right in front of me. He grabbed their hands and put them on my head. Then he recited the ancient ritual formula to make me a rabbi. The two rabbis, stunned, melted back into the crowd. And I—even more stunned—melted back into the crowd.

I went back the next day to Washington, where I was still living. I told Rabbi Max Ticktin what happened. I told him it felt like the *Akedah*, the binding of Isaac. I had no idea what was about to happen, and no choice to be involved. Max looked a little scared, a little nervous. He said, "It's too soon and too sudden. If you claim to be a rabbi, people will not take you seriously and they won't take Zalman seriously." And then he just left me there to think about it.

I did, and then called Zalman on the telephone. "Dear Zalman," I said, "I have been thinking a lot about what happened the night of Shavuot. I think something important did happen. It felt like the binding of Isaac. I didn't know, I wasn't ready. You know my name is Avraham Yitzchak Yishmael. I think my Isaac got *smikha* [ordination]."

But not my Avraham and not my Ishmael. So I won't call myself a rabbi, and I ask you not to. There is too much more I need to grow and learn."

"Are you sure?" he said. "Yes, "I said. He surrendered: "All right then."

I think the Spirit knew there was a dilemma. I think the Spirit approved of the split decision. Indeed, maybe the Spirit put the split decision in my head.

5
Spirit and Person

Early in the history of The Shalom Center, which I founded in 1983 (more on that below), an extraordinary philanthropist and foundation executive, Sidney Shapiro, told me the following story.

> Many years ago, I was the executive director of the Hartford Connecticut Jewish Federation. One day, my secretary came to my door and said, "Mr. Shapiro, there's a gentleman here with a long white beard and a long black coat who says he needs to talk with you."
>
> I said, "Show him in."
>
> The gentleman said to me, "Mr. Shapiro, I need to thank you for saving me from doing such a terrible *aveirah*—a sin."
>
> "What do you mean?"
>
> "I was walking on the street and saw the sign that said 'Hartford Jewish Federation' and I almost walked right past. And then I realized, such a sin it would be for me not to give you the opportunity for you to fulfill the mitzvah, the sacred command to give *tzedakah*—charity."

Said Shapiro to me, "All I could say was, 'How much?!'"

* * *

I first met Esther Ticktin in 1971 at a meeting of the "Jewish Radical Union" of Hillel at the University of Chicago. I was there to ask their support for an action that Jews for Urban Justice in Washington DC (JUJ) wanted to do to confront Judge Julius Hoffman, a Jew who was presiding over the trial of the Chicago Eight, antiwar activists falsely charged by the Nixon Administration with inciting a riot at the Democratic National Convention in Chicago in 1968. In 1971, the Eight were on trial and the judge was acting so hostile and unfair to the defendants that his conviction of them was reversed on appeal for dozens of legal errors he committed.

JUJ had decided that Judge Hoffman must be possessed by a *dybbuk*, an evil spirit—perhaps the Inquisition's Torquemada—for him to be acting this way. So I was sent as a messenger to the Jewish Radical Union in Chicago to ask their support for exorcising Judge Huffman's *dybbuk*.

At the meeting, the first person to speak was a middle-aged woman whom I did not know. She said, "You are proposing to use the Torah scroll in a piece of guerrilla theater!" I said, "We know that the exorcism ritual requires a Torah scroll draped in black with ashes scattered on its covering, but we certainly don't see that as 'guerrilla theater.' Why do you call it that?"

"Because you don't believe in *dybbuks*."

"Why do you think we don't believe in *dybbuks*?"

"If you do, that's superstition!"

So I realized that *Dybbuks* Real or *Dybbuks* Myth, this woman, Esther Ticktin, and her comrades in the Jewish Radical Union opposed the plan. I loved the *chutzpadik* plan for an exorcism, but I've always remembered fondly the down-to-earth-ness of Esther's response.

* * *

In 1975, Martin Buber's tenth *yahrzeit* (anniversary of death) was observed/celebrated in Washington DC by a conference on his teachings that I organized, and that was co-sponsored by Fabrangen, the *havurah* (friendship group, usually for prayer) of which I was a member, and the Institute for Policy Studies, an independent progressive secular think/action center of which I was a resident fellow.

Zalman was one of the speakers. So was Jim Forest, a Berriganian Catholic who was a leader of the Fellowship of Reconciliation. The conference was held on Sunday and Monday. In those days the obligation of Roman Catholics to receive communion each Sunday was quite strong. So on Sunday Zalman approached Jim and asked whether he had a way of receiving communion that morning. Jim said no, and added that he was willing to forego it for the sake of the spiritual depth of the conference.

Zalman then said he considered himself a priest according to the lineage of Melchitzedek, "priest of God Most High, *kohen eyl elyon*" (see Genesis 14:18), and offered to give Jim communion. Jim said yes.

* * *

In the summer of 1986, both my brother and I married our second wives. The wedding that united Phyllis and me was on a farm/retreat center that we had often enjoyed for spirited retreats. Howard and his new bride, Grey Wolfe, stayed overnight after our wedding.

We chatted over breakfast. Howard said to me, "What would you think of writing a book together about what it has been like to be brothers?"

I gulped. This was not so simple. Our brotherhood had been a chilly embrace for most of our lives. That began early: Just a few days after his birth, as we drove to visit my mother—whoops, *our* mother—and infant Howard in the hospital. I discovered there was a major avenue in downtown Baltimore called Howard Street. At three years old, I demanded to see Arthur Street. The grown-ups, laughing, said there was none. Instant envy. And as we grew, on his side was the feeling I was constantly ignoring him, not teaching him.

We had grown closer when "Honey," our mother, went into hospital with lung incapacity in her seventies. The hospital, without consulting her, jammed a respirator in her mouth. She fought against it and fought against the doctors, who claimed under Maryland law in those days it would be murder if they withdrew the respirator.

But the Spirit spoke to Howard and me. They had to disguise their voice with Howard; he was between puzzled and scornful of my religious explorations. "Honor your mother!" they said. So we fought on her side, together at last. And we finally won. The hospital got creative. "Honey" died.

And now, after this checkered past, Howard—who was a skilled family therapist—wanted us to write a book together. "That's your turf!" I finally said. "I would not know where to start or what to say."

Howard nodded, "If you change your mind, let me know."

And then my hearing of the Spirit got blurred. I waited another three or four days, checked in with me and with Spirit. I found, to my surprise, that both they and I were getting more curious what this book might be like. I waited a few more days and then called Howard. "I'm willing." So we did it. We agreed it was about *Becoming Brothers*—changing over the years.

I remember he wrote about our long-ago neighbor Mr. Shapiro's bunions. I said, "Who cares about Mr. Shapiro's bunions?" Howard replied, "Me! *I* care about Mr. Shapiro's bunions." We agreed that the book would be written by each of us, not both of us. Howard would write, I would comment. I would write, Howard would comment.

We heard that on the TV show *Fraser*, the two therapist brothers decided to write a book and tried to agree on every chapter. They revised and revised each other till it ended in a bitter fight, with no book. "We were a lot smarter than Fraser," Howard said. Or the Spirit was, at least for me.

Howard celebrated his seventy-fifth birthday by gathering family and friends from far and near. Then, troubled by pain in mouth and throat, he went to an oncologist. A few days later, he called to tell me the doctors said he had a metastasized, inoperable cancer. He chose not to fight the cancer but to find comfort from pain and sorrow in hospice care. We flew to see him and say goodbye and left him in the loving care of Grey and his sons.

On the night he died, I got a phone call that had no one speaking on the other end. Fifteen minutes later, Grey called to say Howard had breathed his last.

Was the first phone call a breathless last goodbye? A coincidence? A casual wrong number? The Spirit has never breathed me an answer.

* * *

A few months before the U.S. invaded Iraq, together with mostly religious communities, I was involved in raising enough money and enough names of signers and enough words to make up a full-page ad in *The New York Times* urging the U.S. not to invade. My two children who were then in their forties, and who as children at eight and eleven years old had taken part in marches against the U.S. war on Vietnam, both signed the ad.

The *Times* gave us a sizeable discount if we would agree not to know for sure what specific date the ad was going to run. We accepted the discount and the uncertainty.

My son was working in Washington, DC at the time and I knew that he and all his friends would see the *Times* on the exact day the ad appeared. My daughter was a pediatrician in Evanston, Illinois, and it wasn't so clear to me that she would see it right away. So on the day it did appear, I called up to tell her to be sure to get a copy of the *Times* that day. In the middle of the phone conversation, I began to cry. Shoshana asked me, "What's wrong? Why are you crying?" I said, "I thought, like forty years ago when you and David and millions of other people marched against that war, that we had made sure the government would never do that again. But here we are."

Then about a week later, came the day when the city of Philadelphia picked up the recycling and the garbage. The day was cold and rainy and miserable, and I went down to the curb in the chill to pick up the empty garbage cans and take them back to the house. I was muttering to myself, "Every fucking week, you have to pick up the fucking garbage." And then I stood stock still, rain and all, remembering my conversation with Shoshana. I said out loud, "Maybe every generation you have to pick up the fucking garbage." So I felt a little better and a little worse.

On balance, Spirit falling. Do we never get to make real change, deep change, permanent change?

* * *

Once I was being interviewed, about my opposition to the U.S. war in Iraq, by telephone for a radio program in Boston. The interviewer said, "Some people think that opposing the war is unpatriotic. What do you say to that?"

My response was not to say, but to sing, a verse of one of the nation's most loved patriotic songs, emphasizing as I sang the word "patriots."

> O beautiful for patriots' dream
> That sees beyond the years
> Thine alabaster cities gleam
> Undimmed by human tears!
>
> America, America,
> God mend thine every flaw
> Confirm thy good in brotherhood,
> Thy liberty in law.

If I were writing that song, I might slightly change the last two lines: "Confirm thy good in sisterhood, / And international law."

When I was done, there was about half a minute of silence—unheard-of on radio. Then the interviewer said, "You never know when you're going to ask exactly the right question."

* * *

I got a call one morning from a *hazzan* (cantor) at a large synagogue in Philadelphia. He said he needed to talk. I said, "Need? Certainly!" We arranged a date and a time, and he showed up.

"I know that as *hazzan* for the congregation, I'm supposed to be their delegate to God. I'm supposed to communicate their sorrows, their embarrassments, their joys, their sins, to the Holy One, especially on the Yom Kippur that is coming up. But I have a problem. The problem is that I'm gay, and nobody knows it."

I asked, "Are you upset because the Torah and rabbinic halakha are so hostile to gay male Jews, and that feels contradictory to your role as *hazzan*?"

"No, I've settled that for myself. The problem is the secrecy. It feels like my secrecy is standing in the way of being an open channel between the congregation and God."

"Oh. So let me ask you a question. Do you imagine that there is no one in the congregation who is holding tight to a secret that feels dangerous?"

"No, I imagine there are quite a few congregants who are harboring one or another secret that they feel would be disastrous to them if it were revealed."

"So *daven* the secrets, secretly. *Daven* the fear you have about revealing your own secret as the delegate for all the congregants who fear the revealing of their own secrets. You can let them know that's what you're doing, or keep it a secret that that's what you are doing. Either way you are a wonderful channel for all the secret-bearers to the One Who Breathes In and Breathes Out All Secrets."

"Oh. That makes sense. Thanks."

I could hear the Spirit whispering, "I'm not telling."

6
Challenging Power

Writing this book has brought back to me in vivid truth what August 6 meant to me as a child.

On that day in 1946, the first anniversary of the bombing of Hiroshima, I was not quite thirteen years old and was preparing to become a *Bar Mitzvah*—one commanded by God to act as a mature and decent human being.

I was a camper at a Jewish day camp sponsored by "The Y"—the Young Men's and Women's Hebrew Association in Baltimore. I was also editor of its mimeographed weekly newspaper, which we called *The Y's Owl*.

In 1946, August 6 fell on *Tisha B'Av* in the Jewish calendar. The Y directorate was serious about mourning the destruction of both ancient Holy Temples in Jerusalem on that day—at least serious enough to say we could not swim for nine days of grief beforehand.

I wrote my first serious article for that mimeo paper, saying nothing about those ancient Temples. Instead, I wrote that obviously Hiroshima taught us that we must end war. "All these years and failures later, I hope that *a dimly burning wick* [see Isaiah 42:3] will help us bring that memory and that covenant to the foreground of our lives,—mourning the deeply wounded universal Temple—Earth."

On the fiftieth anniversary of the bomb, August 6 again fell on *Tisha B'Av*. By then many American Jews were connecting the two histories. Connecting destruction of the ancient Temples by the Babylonian and

Roman empires. With destruction of Hiroshima by a modern empire and disruption of Earth's climate by arrogant corporations.

The Temples were sacred microcosms of the world. Now the macrocosm—all Earth—may well be destroyed unless we learn to control our arrogant urges to dominate and violate. The Spirit stumbles, falls, and weeps with every species that is killed by corporate human arrogance.

* * *

On July 4, 1963, I was a senior fellow at a tiny research center, the Peace Research Institute. As I had done for a number of years on the 4th, I was rereading the Declaration of Independence when I got a call from Carol Cohen McEldowney. She was my research assistant.

She was calling from Baltimore, asking me to wire money for bail for her and Todd Gitlin, whom I knew, and some other members of Students for a Democratic Society (SDS) who had just been arrested at the Gwynn Oak amusement park in Baltimore, for a racially integrated "walk-in" to end its exclusion of Black folk.

In that park I had danced my senior prom for my all-white, all-male high school in 1950, when like all Baltimore public schools it was formally and legally segregated by race—and remained so till the Supreme Court decision of 1954. And I had danced at Gwynn Oak for my senior prom as I was graduated from Johns Hopkins in 1954. Hopkins was also all-white, except for one Negro student admitted each year in a class of hundreds.

Carol also mentioned, almost casually, that a few days later, on Sunday, July 7, they would be risking arrest again.

After Carol called, for an hour I wrestled with a triple contradiction. One was that Carol and her friends were trying to win integration in my hometown. Seemed like my work more than theirs to do. Secondly, I was ritually reading the Declaration while Carol and the others lived it. And third, I had been involved as a scholar and a legislative assistant in issues of racial equality and civil rights. In July 1963, I was on the verge of completing a doctoral dissertation in U.S. history for the University of Wisconsin—a dissertation I'd begun five years before, about a series of race riots. My legislative work from 1959 to 1961 had supported a congressman who was a member of the House Judiciary Committee, which was struggling over draft civil rights legislation.

So what was I doing sitting in Washington while they were inviting arrest in my hometown, upholding my Declaration of Independence, on issues I had written about?

I called a psychiatrist friend who had done important research with the early sit-inners in the South, to talk out my uncertainty. After fifteen minutes he said, "Arthur, sounds to me like you've made up your mind already what to do." I had. I decided to take part in the Sunday arrests.

On Sunday morning, I went to Baltimore. I began by taking the last chapter of my race-riot dissertation to my mother, for her to type. University rules were that a dissertation had to be letter-perfect. If there was a typing error, the whole page had to be retyped. I was a terrible typist; my mother, an excellent one.

Then I went to the Metropolitan African Methodist Episcopal Church, where the protesters were gathering. When I got there, Carol and Todd took me aside. "We're bored by this ritual arrest process at the front entrance of the amusement park," they said. "The cops and the owner draw a line in the dirt, we walk across it, and we're arrested for trespass. We've discovered there's a back way into the park, across a tiny stream. We'd like to do it that way, actually get into the park itself, take a ride on the merry-go-round before they arrest us. Actually integrate the place. Are you game?"

I knew no one else. "Sure," I said.

When we arrived at the stream, I took off my shoes. (The others, a lot younger and less stuffy than I, did not.) We walked into the park.

But we had not taken into account that on July 5, the Baltimore newspapers had headlined the protests on Independence Day and announced there would be another wave on the 7th. So hundreds of diehard segregationists had gathered in the park, ready to defend their turf against us "niggers, nigger-lovers, and commies."

We learned they were there when a huge chunk of concrete, flung by a young mother with a child at her side, caught our co-protester Alison Turaj on the side of her face. She began bleeding profusely. Then a crowd appeared, screaming at us, running toward us, surrounding us, pushing, yelling.

As I stood there, my mind ran through my dissertation about those race riots long ago. I knew this scenario. They yelled, they pushed, they threw things—and when somebody fell down, they killed you. *I am living inside my dissertation*, I thought. At that moment, the police appeared. They had no interest in threats, in violence, in rock-throwing. They arrested us—for trespass. They probably saved our lives.

Our march to the arrest wagon brought us past some of the same cotton candy stands and thrill rides that I could remember from when I danced at Gwynn Oak fifteen years before. I felt utterly pierced by the knowledge that this was my Baltimore, the mob my fellow Baltimoreans, showing me hatred that I had never had to face, but that Baltimore Negroes must have faced for all their lives. We were singing the verse from "We Shall Overcome": "We are not afraid." Our voices were quavering. We were afraid. But we were also joyful. We had challenged and been challenged. Courage was acting despite fear, not without it.

An Associated Press photographer caught the moment as we moved under arrest. The photo appeared the next morning on the front page of the *Baltimore Sun*.* For ten years, Blacks had been demonstrating, boycotting, and going to court about the segregation of Gwynn Oak. They had brought the city to the edge of change. I heard that the blood on Alison's face—the wound required twelve stitches and endangered her eye—became, for the "moderate" leaders of Baltimore, the final drop in the rainstorm.

---

* *Those in the photo include Alison Turaj, with blood streaming down her face and staining her dress; to Alison's right, Carol Cohen McEldowney; to her right, Todd Gitlin, now a well-known sociologist at Columbia University, whose book on the Sixties has a passage on the Gwynn Oak arrests; and to Alison's left, me, with shoes in hand.*

They insisted that the county executive of Baltimore County, Spiro Agnew, enter into negotiations with the owner of the park. On August 28, the same day as the Great March For Jobs And Freedom in Washington DC at which Dr. King gave his "I have a dream" speech, an African-American child rode on the Gwynn Oak merry-go-round, no longer a "trespasser."

That summer, I wrote an essay on the arrests that appeared originally as an article in *The Saturday Review*. It was later published as the opening chapter of my 1970 book, *Running Riot: A Journey Through the Official Disasters and Creative Disorder of American Society*. Here are excerpts from that essay.

> Why Jail?
>
> If I feel that scholarship and writing are important tasks for me to keep on with (and I do), what place should something like civil disobedience have in my life? Scientists get exempted from the military draft; should intellectuals be exempted from nonviolent (but risky) protest? Ultimately, I decided it is dishonest to urge without undertaking, and impossible to understand without acting.
>
> I was prepared to go back to Gwynn Oak. But the business community of Baltimore was upset by a front-page newspaper photo of Alison profusely bleeding. They feared it gave the impression their city was anarchic. So they leaned heavily on Gov. Spiro Agnew and he on the owners of Gwynn Oak, until they agreed to integrate the park.
>
> I scarcely decided to be on the picket lines every Sunday. But where an event reached out to touch my life again as this one did, I did not stay at my desk.

Now, a note from sixty years later: The last line of this article was in fact prescient. Gwynn Oak was for me the first of about twenty-eight arrests in various protests. The most recent was as part of an interfaith group challenging the U.S. president to act more vigorously on the climate crisis, on Independence Mall on my 89th birthday—October 12, 2022, sixty years after Gwynn Oak.

The county executive of Baltimore County who ordered our arrest in 1963, Spiro Agnew, was later elected governor of Maryland and vice-president of the U.S. under Richard Nixon. In 1973, he resigned that office in disgrace, charged with bribery and extortion during his tenure of all three offices.)

I can't end this note without honoring the memory of one of my comrades in the arrest—Carol Cohen McEldowney, my research assistant, who called me on that evening of July 4 to ask me to post bail for some of those who had been arrested at Gwynn Oak. Carol went on to do powerful activist work in a neighborhood of poverty-stricken whites in Cleveland, to take part in an illegal antiwar visit by American activists to Hanoi during the Vietnam War, and then to play an important part in the women's movement in Boston. She was killed in a car crash in 1973. Her *Hanoi Journal, 1967* was published in 2007 by the University of Massachusetts Press. Her life was a model of compassion and commitment; her death, a loss to us all.

* * *

My second arrest, like the first, was on the issue of racism: international racism, the opposite of my hometown amusement park.

In 1965, hundreds of people—many of us students at Union Theological Seminary in New York City—gathered on the steps of the Chase Manhattan Bank to demand that they stop investing in South Africa. It was the first in what became a worldwide storm of the Spirit that finally toppled South African Apartheid.

We were all arrested for blocking the bank's customers from entering, and taken off to Police Precinct Number 1.

I was amazed at how clean and tidy the cell block was—very different from the cells in Baltimore two years earlier. I admired the cleanliness to the police captain at the desk. "Yes," he said, "nobody gets arrested on Wall Street."

Oh, I thought. *Nobody gets arrested; but there are plenty of crimes on Wall Street.* I stored that away as a wisdom for the future.

※ ※ ※

In 1966, the Methodist Student Movement held its national gathering in Washington, DC. Young people from around the country were beginning to question the US War against Vietnam, and the young Methodists asked the Institute for Policy Studies for a briefing on the war. The Institute sent me.

I analyzed the war from a moral perspective, and then there were a number of questions. Finally, one college student asked, "We get what you think of the war. What would you do about it?"

I answered, "There's a photo in my head that I imagine comes from the front page of the *New York Times*. It's the result of a confrontation between police and students who have come with crosses and Torah scrolls to block the entrance to a factory that makes napalm—jellied gasoline to burn Vietnamese to death. The crosses and Torah scrolls are scattered in the street, strewn there when the police attacked the protesters."

"Okay, but why the cross?" said one Methodist student.

I was silent for quite an interval. Then I said, "If I, a Jewish kid from Baltimore, have to explain 'why the cross,' I guess western civilization is over."

There was a longer silence. Then one of the students said, "Many of us see the cross as just a commercial ad at those empty pillboxes on the corner."

A still longer silence. I said, "You will have to decide that, not me." I stood up and left. The Spirit stayed behind, waiting to hear the answer to the question.

※ ※ ※

By the High Holy Days of 1969, *The Freedom Seder* was still controversial but had already shown compelling attractive power. So Rabbi Nathan Abramowitz of Tiferet Israel, a Conservative shul in uptown Washington DC, had a bright idea: On Yom Kippur, he would lead the conventional prayers in the official sanctuary, and he would invite me and other younger or less conventional folk to create a service downstairs, in a large social hall. Of course, I said yes.

I set to work to learn what the traditional forms might open themselves in order to go deeper into redeeming the messier parts of American society. "The *Al Chet*, for example: Could this recitation of "the misdeeds we have mis-done in Your face" include social sins like racism and war and slumlord exploitation of poverty-stricken tenants?

And of course I notified Jews for Urban Justice, asking them to come and to invite their friends.

Meanwhile, the rabbi was having trouble. Some of the "upstairs" conventional folks were angry that the board had not been consulted. They demanded my plans be reviewed by the board. I agreed, and in person I presented my plans. I included two special requests: first, that the U.S. flag be discreetly removed from the platform. One board member shouted, "Next the Israeli flag, huh?" I answered calmly, "So far as I know, the Israeli government is not napalming Palestinians. The U.S. government is napalming Vietnamese. Anyway, it's just a request. Do what you want."

Secondly, I asked that everyone be given the time to read the new *Al Chet* before choosing to recite it, and that only those who agreed with it be asked to stand and read it. I had in mind protecting the war-supporters from being singled out. Some of the board were more interested in not singling out supporters of the war; they suggested getting everyone to stand by opening the Ark. I said it was up to them.

Yom Kippur itself was even tenser. My sermon said that just as Jonah refused God's call to prophesy to the sinners of Nineveh, the American Jewish community was refusing God's call to prophesy to the American people and government. Some people booed. Then, a member of the congregation stood up and said, "I am a rabbi!" Everybody quieted down to hear the voice of authority. He was Rabbi Alan Lettofsky. "Many of you seem to think Yom Kippur is a day to enjoy yourselves. Just the opposite! It is a day, Torah says, to afflict your souls, to press down your egos. Waskow is doing a great job of asking you to do that. Listen to him!" More people listened, but there was more angst to come.

The worst moment came with the recitation of the *Al Chet*. When the service began, a synagogue official had told me that the "conventional visitors" upstairs objected to opening the Ark for the *Al Chet*, so the board was confirming their wishes. I shrugged: "Wasn't my idea. Up to the board." When the moment came, however, the Tiferet member who had been told to open the Ark ... did! Nobody had told him not to. The "conventionals" thought they'd been betrayed. They charged the sacred Ark and forced it closed. Then they came for me, but the Jews for Urban Justice people, echoing civil-rights practice, encircled me and clasped hands, protecting me.

Their charging leader yelled, "This will never happen in this synagogue again!" A JUJ member yelled back, "You will lose all your young people!" Then he topped her: "I don't care! I paid for this synagogue, and it will never happen here again!"

Afterward, the synagogue appointed a commission to investigate who was responsible for "the Yom Kippur riot." It investigated me, the preferred target, but couldn't find anything I did wrong. They investigated the officially convicted slumlord who said he paid for the synagogue, but didn't dare find anything he did wrong. Finally, they chose to blame Rabbi Abramowitz for guessing wrong that the conventional folks would stay upstairs with him, not descend to the nether pits of holiness to make trouble. But they didn't fire him. Meanwhile, the Spirit was giddy, dancing in joy, weeping in sorrow, and gnashing teeth in anger that us poor Yom Kippur fasters all thought They were on our side.

* * *

There was a briefcase with 1,000 "illegal" draft cards that we gave the Department of Justice. But, as it turned out, the FBI was eavesdropping outside the door of the room where we turned them in.

The FBI grabbed the briefcase, carefully checked each card, and sent it to the draft board where it originated. It would warn them that somebody was "illegally" walking around without his card in his pocket.

So I heard from my old draft board in Baltimore that I had been reclassified from 4F (physically or emotionally unsuitable for military service) to IA (immediately draftable). I could appeal.

I appealed and agreed on a date when I would appear in Baltimore before the draft board. I told a reporter at the *Washington Star* and he agreed it could be a juicy story. We drove to Baltimore.

When I introduced him to the board as my friend whom I'd like to have sit in the hearing, they said no. No outsiders, to protect the privacy of each draftable guy. "But the rules are to protect me, and I'm asking he be admitted!" Still no.

OK. I was prepared to present my statement. But they insisted on speaking first. The chairman said, "If we return your card, will you promise to carry it as legally required? If so, we will reclassify you 4F." "I am entitled to appeal, and I have a statement of appeal!"

"Just answer the question. Will you promise to carry the card?"

"My answer is in my statement."

"No, we need your answer now."

In my own briefcase was a tape recorder. I pulled it out, put it on the table, and pushed the start button.

"You can't do that! Turn it off!"

"Who says I can't?"

"There's a rule!" Turning to the draft board secretary, who was not a member of the board, and who was also the only woman in the room, I said, "Go find the rule!" She disappeared to look it up.

Meanwhile, the recorder was buzzing and spinning. My God! The key piece, which takes in voices and records them, was missing! I fumbled in my briefcase. Nothing. Then I just sat there, dazed but silent.

The secretary returned. "I cannot find any rule about tape recorders," she said.

The board and I sat eyeing each other, stymied. And then I made a magnanimous offer. "I'll turn off my recorder and put it away if you will let me make my statement of appeal."

A deep sigh came from the chairman. "OK."

So I dumped the useless recorder back in my briefcase and made my brief statement, condemning the war as immoral and illegal, refusing to carry the draft card, invoking the Nuremberg anti-Nazi ruling that every citizen of a nation that is violating the laws of humanity is obligated to resist its government's violation, and ended by urging the board to resign. "That is the basis of my appeal," I said, and "I await your decision."

I waited quite a while. The law provided that no one could be drafted after turning thirty-five. Shortly after my thirty-fifth birthday, I received a letter from the Baltimore draft board. They had reviewed my appeal and restored my 4F.

I joined the *Ruach*—Holy Spirit, Wind of change, Breath of life, in a sigh of relief and a laugh of joy.

* * *

Every year on Thanksgiving, WXPN Radio in Philadelphia (and many other radio stations around the country) play Arlo Guthrie's song "Alice's Restaurant." It's about a Thanksgiving dinner in Stockbridge Massachusetts in 1967; about obtuse cops; and about nonviolent resistance to a brutal war. And every year, in a flurry of phone calls around our neighborhood, several other men and I fulfill our own ancient Thanksgiving ritual, calling to make sure we are all tuned in. We—a bunch of rabbis and a Jewish Renewal foundation executive turned Zohar teacher had been members of a men's group that met each week since 1983.

Every year, this seemingly non-Jewish set of rituals stirs in me the memory of a moment long ago when my first puzzled, uncertain explorations of the Jewish thing took on new power for me. And when I came to understand the power of a *yarmulke*.

In 1970, I was asked by the Chicago Eight to testify in their defense. They were leaders of the movement to oppose the Vietnam War, and they had been charged by the U.S. government (i.e. the Nixon Administration and Attorney-General John Mitchell, who turned out to be a criminal himself) with conspiracy to organize riot and destruction during the Chicago Democratic National Convention (DNC) in 1968.

I had been an alternate delegate from the District of Columbia to the Convention—elected originally as part of an anti-war, anti-racist slate to support Robert Kennedy. After he was murdered, we decided to nominate and support the chairperson of our delegation—Rev. Channing Phillips, a Black minister in the Martin Luther King, Jr. mold. Our delegation made him the first Black person ever nominated for president at a major-party convention. The following spring, on the first anniversary of Dr. King's murder, on the third night of Pesach in 1969, his church hosted the first-ever Freedom Seder.

I had spoken the first two nights of the convention to the anti-war demonstrators at Grant Park, at their invitation, while the crowd was being menaced by Chicago police and the National Guard. And the police had exploded in violence on the third night, when the crowd tried to march peacefully toward the convention as the delegates began voting on presidential candidates.

Although the official investigation described it as a "police riot," the Nixon Administration decided to indict the anti-war leaders. So during the 1970 trial of Tom Hayden, David Dellinger, Abby Hoffman, et al. I figured I would be reasonably respectable (as a former delegate) and therefore convincing to the jury and the national public, testifying that the anti-war folks were not trying to organize violence, but were instead the victims of police violence.

As the trial went forward, it became clear that the judge, Julius Hoffman, a Jew, was utterly subservient to the prosecution and wildly hostile to the defense. Judge Hoffman browbeat witnesses, and gagged and bound Bobby Seale, the only Black defendant in the courtroom, for challenging his rulings. Dozens of his rulings against the Eight were later cited by the Court of Appeals as major legal errors, requiring reversal of all the convictions the prosecution had achieved in his court.

When I arrived at the Federal courthouse in Chicago, I was very nervous—about the judge, more than the prosecution or my own testimony.

The witness who was scheduled to testify right before me was Arlo Guthrie. He had sung "Alice's Restaurant" to/with the crowd at Grant Park, and the defense wanted to show the jury that there was no incitement to violence in it. So William Kunstler, the lawyer for the defense, asked Guthrie to sing the song so that the jury could get a direct sense of the event. But Judge Hoffman stopped him: "You can't sing in my courtroom!"

"But," said Kunstler, "it is evidence of the intent of the organizers and the crowd!" And for minutes they snarled at each other. Finally, Judge Hoffman acquiesced slightly. "He can *say* what he told them, but *no singing*."

But then, Guthrie couldn't do it. The song, which lasts twenty-five minutes, he knew by heart, having sung it more than a thousand times—but to say it without singing, he couldn't. His memory was keyed to the melody. And maybe Judge Hoffman's rage helped disassemble him. So he came back to the witness room, crushed.

I was up next. I started trembling, trying to figure out how I could avoid falling apart.

I decided that if I wore a *yarmulke*, that would strengthen me to connect with a power Higher/Other than the United States and Judge Hoffman. Up to that moment, I had never worn a *yarmulke* in a non-officially "religious" situation. I had written *The Freedom Seder* in 1969 but was in 1970 still wrestling with the question of what this weird and powerful Jewish thing meant in my life.

I told Kunstler I wanted to wear a *yarmulke*, and he said, "No problem." Somewhere I found a simple black, unobtrusive skull-cap, and when I went to be sworn in, I put it on. For the oath—which I did as an affirmation, as indicated by much of Jewish tradition—was no problem. Then Kunstler asked me the first question for the defense, and the judge interrupted. "Take off your hat, sir," he said.

To which Kunstler erupted. "This man is an Orthodox Jew, and you want—" etc. etc. etc. I was moaning to myself, *Please, Bill, one thing I know I'm not is an Orthodox Jew*. But how can I undermine the defense attorney? So I kept my mouth shut.

Judge Hoffman erupted again: "That hat shows disrespect for the United States and this Honorable Court!" *Yeah, I think to myself, that's sort-of true. Disrespect for him, absolutely. For the United States, not disrespect, exactly, but much more respect for Something Else. That's the point!*

They kept yelling, and I started watching the prosecutor. And I realized that he was watching the jury. There was one Jewish juror. What was this juror thinking?

Finally, the prosecutor addressed the judge: "Your Honor, the United States certainly understands and agrees with your concern, but we also feel that in the interests of justice, it might be best simply for the trial to go forward." And the judge took orders! He shut up, and the rest of my testimony was quiet and orderly.

It took me another year or so to start wearing some sort of hat all the time.

For years, it was a Tevye cap. For years, and some of the time now, a beret. Sometimes a rainbow *kippah*. Sometimes in a rough winter, an amazing tall Tibetan hat with earflaps and wool trimming that I found in a Tibetan Buddhist harvest festival that came right during *Sukkot* (when else?). Whatever its shape, the hat continues to mean to me that there is a Higher, Deeper Truth in the world than any judge, any attorney general, or any pharaoh.

Maybe "Alice's Restaurant" was Arlo's *yarmulke*.

✳ ✳ ✳

It was *Tisha B'Av* 1972—the scorching hot midsummer day when Jews mourn the destruction of two Holy Temples in Jerusalem, one by the Babylonian Empire 2,500 years ago; the second, by the Roman Empire 2,000 years ago. For twenty-five hours, observant Jews fast from food, water, sex, taking baths, even leather shoes.

In Washington, DC, a small, vibrant, independent-minded, and creative group that called ourselves Jews for Urban Justice was fasting on the steps of the U.S. Capitol. Why? Because the Senate was considering whether to ratify a treaty with the Soviet Union to ban anti-ballistic missiles. The treaty was intended to protect the world against a nuclear arms race that could, if the weapons were used, shatter life on the planet.

That felt to JUJ like a danger not just to one sacred site but to the universal temple that we call Earth. A danger posed by the two great Empires of that generation—the United States and the Soviet Union. The Soviets wanted the treaty; the U.S. Senate was not so sure. So we were bringing the spiritual meaning of *Tisha B'Av* to bear as a Jewish voice urging the Senate to ratify the treaty. (A few days later, they did.)

We had a separate quarrel with the Soviet Union. Its government was harassing and oppressing Soviet Jews. So on this *Tisha B'Av*, we also decided to demonstrate at the Soviet Embassy.

The District had a law prohibiting demonstrations within 500 feet of an embassy—a law passed to inhibit Jewish demonstrations against the Nazi government of Germany in the 1930s. So the established Jewish organizations of Washington were demonstrating against the Soviet government's treatment of Jews, but they were demonstrating in front of an airline office 500 feet away.

After our vigil at the Senate, we joined that demonstration. But after fifteen minutes, we realized that to us it felt ridiculous to be picketing an innocent airline instead of the Soviet Embassy itself. We moved 500 feet up 16th Street. We began walking a picket line in front of the embassy. After another fifteen minutes, someone came out of the embassy. He said, "You go 'way or I call po-lees."

In my best Sixties *chutzpah*, I responded, "Strange that the Soviet Socialist Republics would call the capitalist police."

He answered, "Meks no diff'rence. This private prropporrty. You go 'way or I call po-lees."

"This is private property?" I said. But I knew it. An empire is an empire, no matter its label. We kept picketing.

Fifteen minutes more, and two policemen showed up. I was on the embassy steps at this point, and decided that if we were going to be forced to stop, I at least wanted our message to reach the embassy. So I pressed the doorbell, intending to give them our picket signs. But the policeman began shouting, "Don't go in! Don't go in! Inside is their territory, they can do whatever they like, we can't intervene."

The door buzzed. I could have gone in, but I was shaken by their warning. So I opened the door, tossed all the picket signs into the front hall, pulled the door closed, and walked back down to the pavement and the police. "You're under arrest," one of them then said.

"For what?" I said.

"Littering in a public place," said he.

Off we went to the nearest police precinct. Its lead officer told me I had two choices: Post $15 in lieu of a fine, or schedule a trial. "First," I said, "Can I call a lawyer?" Sure. So I called the Washington office of the American Civil Liberties Union, explained the drama I was in, said I thought the 500-feet rule was unconstitutional, and asked for a lawyer.

A big belly-laugh came from the guy on the phone. "Mr. Waskow, every lawyer in DC is right now in Rehoboth, Delaware, swimming in the Atlantic." Muttering curses under my breath, I went back to the desk, took $15 out of my pocket, and paid it. Soviet Union 1, U.S. Constitution 0. The Spirit, laughing at us all.

* * *

In the mid-1970s, Senator Frank Church led a senatorial investigation of the behavior of the FBI and other government law enforcement groups toward the constantly growing movement to end the

U.S. war against Vietnam. His committee discovered that FBI agents had created not just secret investigations of legal meetings and conversations of antiwar people, but were actually breaking the laws themselves. They had stolen mail, forged documents, and disrupted meetings. In some cases—like Fred Hampton of the Black Panthers in Chicago—they had murdered grassroots leaders. This effort was called the co-intel-pro operation (for counter-intelligence program), and it was approved by J. Edgar Hoover himself, the FBI director.

In Washington, where I was living, a cluster of nine people of all sorts of backgrounds who had opposed the war with strong energy decided to bring suit against the FBI for violating the First Amendment to the Constitution, especially freedom of association and assembly. I was one of the nine. We sued to get the records from FBI files. They were astonishing, grim, and sometimes ludicrous.

For instance, a student of mine at the institute for Policy Studies, Jeremy Brecher, sent me a paper he had written, arguing that a socialist transformation of America was possible. He sent it as a Xerox paper. But his Xerox machine was running out of paper, and automatically printed on the back of each sheet something to warn the writer that it needed a new sheaf of paper to be fed into the machine. The message on the back of each sheet said something like "paper running out." Jeremy, in his cover letter to me, joked, "Be sure to decode the secret cryptogram on the back of the Xerox sheets."

The letter came through the mail with his article and it got put in my mailbox at the Institute. But the FBI had a local paid informant in Washington, who evidently came in one day and stole everything out of my post office box to give the FBI. All this turned up in the papers that the FBI turned over to us when we sued. There was a cover memo from the FBI for Jeremy's letter and its paper, and the xerox pages with their secret code. It said, "We have spent weeks trying to decode the secret words and sent them to a cryptographer, but he is unable to make any sense out of it."

That is the ludicrous part of the work we were doing then.

But there was lots more. Most of it was horrifying, and only a little was ludicrous. We were able to show ordinary citizens in the jury what the FBI was actually doing in the co-intel-pro operation. We did not claim any financial loss; we only claimed hurt and damages from being denied our right to free assembly and our right to be able to carry on a political effort without disruption by the U.S. government.

The jury agreed that this was an invasion of our rights that was absolutely worth financial redress. They awarded the nine of us almost a total of a million dollars.

The FBI, of course, appealed. The Circuit Court for Washington, DC upheld the basic verdict, but said the financial award was too great. They sent it back for the lower court to work out. We ended up with enough that each of us received about $9,000 rather than $90,000.

I divided my $9,000 into three parts. The lawsuit took so long that by the time the final award was decided, there was an internet run by computers that you could get on an office desk. A good computer cost about $3,000 and I set aside that much to buy one to use in the work of The Shalom Center. To each of my children, who were then eighteen and twenty-one years old, I said: "Ordinarily we couldn't afford for you to spend the year with no one able to support you in the doing. But because of this lawsuit, I can offer you $3,000 if you want to spend the year doing change-oriented activism. It's up to you. If you would rather pursue a regular job, that's fine. But if you would like to start your working life with political action, you can have a fellowship to do it." Each of them said yes. David chose to do tenants' rights organizing in Massachusetts. Shoshana chose to work at a women's retreat center for survivors of domestic violence who had fled their abusers and needed protection and community. I told them there was just one condition. This grant would be named the "J. Edgar Hoover Memorial Fellowship" and I hoped they would remember how and why they got it. Nearly fifty years later and they still remember.

* * *

An owner of a crucial stand of ancient redwoods in northern California was Jewish, and much more than casually Jewish. He lived in Houston, was a mainstay of a Houston Reform temple, and sent slews of money to a very conservative religious Jewish institution in Israel.

Various Jews had spent years trying to persuade him to stop logging the ancient redwoods, but they could get no response. In 1997, led by Rabbi Naomi Steinberg, they performed a magical publicity coup by naming a group of northern California rabbis the "Redwood Rabbis." That gave them an attractive jumping-off place to approach him yet again. They wrote rabbis all over the country, imploring them to join the "Redwood Rabbis" and dozens—then, hundreds—said yes.

They decided to ask as many of them as could to come to California on *Tu B'Shvat* (the festival that not only celebrates the rebirth of trees each spring but sees the whole world as the Divine Tree of Life). They would gather and hold a *Tu B'Shvat* seder in a federally-owned and protected stand of ancient redwoods and then proceed from there to the redwood property that was being logged. They would walk onto the exploited land carrying baby redwoods to replace ones that had been killed. The expectation was that the owner would send both the public police and hired security forces to arrest them all.

First, we gathered for what was a joyful seder in the midst of the forest of protected redwoods. I was sitting next to Naomi Mara Hyman, a rabbinical student in the ALEPH ordination program. She leaned over and said, "We call these trees *eytzim*, right?" I answered, "Yes, we do." "And," she continued, "we call the poles made of wood that hold the two ends of the spiral of the Torah scroll, we also call them *eyztim*, right?" "Yes," I said, feeling the Spirit beginning to pay attention.

"So what would happen if we imagine a Torah scroll that was tall enough and big enough for these great ancient redwood *eytzim* to be the *eytzim* holding that *Sefer Torah*? Would our imaginations be large enough to imagine such a Torah? And what about each one of us sitting around the table for this wonderful seder? Are we big enough to be, each one of us, one letter in that expansive Torah? What if every Shabbat we reminded ourselves that we are letters in God's great Torah, responsible to stay well-defined and well-connected?"

"Wonderful!" I said, "I notice that nowhere in the Torah does a single letter stand alone. In your wonderfully imagined *Sefer Torah*, we don't sit here alone with the great redwood *eytzim* around us. We all make the words of wisdom by linking ourselves to each other. Thank you, Naomi. I can already hear the Spirit singing a song about trees and you've made me feel much stronger about liberating the trees that we're going to visit very soon."

So we packed up the seder, and walked about a mile carrying baby redwoods. We could see the police and the hired security close to the edge of the property line, ready to arrest us when we crossed it. But then they began to move. They evidently had gotten orders to pull back. For the redwood owner, the embarrassment of dozens of arrests of us trying to save the redwoods was greater than the embarrassment of letting outside agitators on his property.

Still, the pressure to save the redwoods didn't stop there. The Redwood Rabbis placed an ad in the Houston Jewish newspaper before Yom Kippur. The owner's family tried to get the paper to refuse the ad, but the family-owned paper—not owned like many others by the local Jewish Federation—were independent enough to run it anyway.

Then came a meeting of stockholders in the corporation that owned the redwoods being logged. The religiously rooted council for corporate responsibility bought a few ownership shares in the redwood corporation and invited me to be one of those that carried them to the stockholder meeting, where I got to speak as a proxy stockholder about the policy of logging ancient redwoods. I showed up, full of piss and vinegar, to say my piece and cast my ballot. Somebody figured out who I was and sent someone to talk with me who they thought could calm me down—a member of the corporate board and also a trustee of the Jewish Theological Seminary. He said, "I don't know if you have heard, we have started a program of placing redwood seedlings wherever we log the ancient trees. So we are constantly replenishing the stock."

I said, "Suppose I told you I owned the great stones of the Western Wall in Jerusalem and I was selling them, one by one, because they would bring in a lot of money, and I was replacing them with new stones, small stones, what would you say?"

"I would say that's a problem. I would say it corrupts the holiness of the Wall."

"I can hear the Holy Spirit turning somersaults. It is the same thing as your program for the redwoods. Those magnificent ancient redwoods are holy! If you are imagining that I will shut up, nothing doing."

It took a couple more years but the corporation finally made a deal to turn over most of its ancient redwood stand to the State of California and the federal government and got out of the business of logging ancient trees. The Spirit, which had started rising the instant that the police pulled back, chanted halleluyah!

* * *

On March 29, 2003, the U.S. government under the second President Bush invaded the Republic of Iraq. It claimed that Iraq had a nuclear weapons program that was threatening the Middle East and for that matter, the world. The United Nations had serious nuclear investigators in Iraq, and they were reporting they could see no evidence of a nuclear arsenal or a nuclear weapons program. But major U.S. media believed the liars in the U.S. government, and so the U.S. Army was stationed, ready to invade.

All around the world there were large demonstrations against the war. One of them was in Washington, DC, and I was determined to take part. The plan was to gather in Lafayette Park, right across Pennsylvania Avenue from the White House. Many of the demonstrators were bitterly hostile to the police who were prepared to clear the park, if necessary, with tear gas and arrests. But I thought of the police as victims of the war. I decided, for the first time in all my arrests, to try to talk with them.

I brought a bullhorn and pointed it at the nearest contingent of police. "Officers, I would be glad to have your attention for just a couple of minutes. We know that you are just on the verge of arresting or even tear gassing some of us. We realize that you are doing this because you understand that your duty is to clear this park so people will want to picnic here or just sit and enjoy the sunshine.

"We realize that our presence, even though we are sure it is protected by the Constitution, is keeping the ordinary use of the park from happening. And we understand that this seems to you a small but real legal offense. So we understand your feelings, your thoughts, and what are about to be your actions.

"But we want to call your attention to much worse legal offenses—in fact, federal and international crimes—that are already being committed in that big white house over there and will be committed by their orders to kill human beings in Iraq. We ask you to remember that just as you are police, you are also American citizens who care about big crimes as well as little crimes.

"You are citizens of the world who care about other human beings who live in this world of many nations. We invite you to keep that in mind. If it is too much of a strain to keep it in mind while arresting us, please keep it in mind when you are with your families, when you are having lunch, when you are having a weekend or a vacation to relax in."

The police said nothing. But we could see they heard.

***

Some years ago, The Shalom Center gathered just outside the nuclear weapons testing center in the Nevada desert. We decided to hold a pre-Passover Seder there to challenge the danger of a nuclear holocaust, what we called "the Final Pharaoh." After the seder, we intended to walk onto the test-site itself and be arrested for trespass, to protest the nuclear arms race and its threat of nuclear holocaust.

Halfway through the seder, one of the celebrants suddenly pointed at the sky and said, "Look!" There was a rainbow. In that desert there had been no rain for many many months—perhaps years. "Unheard of!" came the murmurings around their circle. "A miracle!" "God's blessing on our protest!"

As we left afterward, walking toward the official boundary of the test-site so as to be arrested, one of our community beckoned me aside. "Optically," he said, "grains of sand and dust in the desert air act like raindrops to diffract white sunlight into the colors of the rainbow."

I smiled and said, "Optically, it was a miracle."

* * *

One of the most important risings of the Spirit remains in my memory as a major teaching of how very different communities can work together and change their own understanding in the process. This started with an invitation to join in a demonstration in south Philadelphia against a massive concentration of oil refineries there. I went to uphold The Shalom Center's efforts to save planet Earth from climate chaos. What I saw when I got to south Philadelphia was human harmony, for a neighborhood and a planet of harmony.

I saw large groups of Black folk just outside the refinery fence, with signs about asthma and cancer, mixed with large groups of white people at the main gate of the refinery complex, carrying signs about climate craziness: wildfires, floods, famine.

Both groups blocked the one road into the refinery district, cutting it off from the surrounding world as its bosses had cut caring about the surrounding world, both neighborly and planetary, from their "possessive-property" interest in the refineries.

I saw the neighborly Blacks and the planetary whites swirling in a wonderful stew, with the Spirit as a delicious sauce.

The Black neighborhood turned out with all its cultural expression becoming activists. An all-Black marching band in bright yellow uniforms plus majorettes twirling batons led a parade of neighbors to block the intersection that led to the refinery complex. There they joined mostly-white climate activists on happy high-fives as business traffic screeched to a baffled halt. "Philly Thrive" from the Black neighborhoods unveiled dozens of giant hand-painted sunflowers. On each was inscribed the name of a neighbor who in the community's judgment had died early from disease caused by the refineries' poisoning of the air.

I was joyful that as an elder I was invited to speak to the crowd. I drew on the ancient story of the Exodus, probably as well known to many in the Black neighborhood as it was to many of the Jewish activists who were taking part. I spoke of the modern pharaohs who were poisoning people and planet in order to accumulate hyper-wealth for themselves. To do this, they were bringing on the modern plagues of heart and lung diseases, tempests and floods. Living through both struggles brought both groups to see that not-caring about the health of close neighbors and not-caring about the health of all Earth were closely related in the behavior of refinery bosses—mostly because caring for others would lessen their hyper-wealth.

The strongly Black "Philly Thrive," led by three "founding mothers"—Sylvia Bennett, Carol Hemingway, and Carol White—and the strongly white "Green Justice Philly," led by Rabbi Mordechai Liebling, Matt Walker, and Tracy Carluccio—both went through changes into full eco-consciousness where their alliance became profoundly shared, not just casually useful. The two groups joined in that wonderful stew where they saw their interests and their visions semi-merging.

Afterward I spoke with a Black clergyman, Rev. Greg Holston. He was then head of POWER, a multiracial, multireligious amalgam of congregations striving to make a Philadelphia where everyone could thrive. He said his kids grew up in the neighborhood close to the refineries. One of them spent anxious days in hospital almost every year, coughing her lungs out with asthma. He thought her illness was God's inscrutable will until they moved across the bridge to southern New Jersey and her asthma magically ended. "That was the first time I knew the meaning of environmental injustice," he said, ruefully laughing. "The label on the prescription bottle for curing the plague said 'Action for environmental justice.' But this Rx didn't come from the neighborhood drugstore. We had to work for it, struggle for it, block streets for it."

We were able to bring his insight to a wider multiracial mingling by having him speak at the fiftieth anniversary of the original Freedom Seder, held by The Shalom Center. Only a few years later, the refineries provided their own explosive ending. Literally, they exploded. Miraculously, no one got hurt. Perhaps the Spirit blew an extraordinary swift response into a refinery worker. She quickly pushed the right button to prevent the explosion from pouring toxic gas over the neighborhood.

And the slow deaths ended. The slow deaths inflicted by the refineries on the neighborhood through lung disease and cancer—they ended. The company that owned the ravaged wreck tried to revive the oil business by making the Port of Philadelphia an export center for oil and liquefied gas, but the neighborhood and its climate-activist allies had bonded too strongly to let that happen. And the holy Spirit blew as a wind of strength to shield the people and the planet.

Everyone who protested understood that the union of anti-racist and acceptance of women as leaders and anti-corporate care for Earth had connected into a shared struggle. And that it was valuable to follow Black women as frontline leaders who were most directly harmed by the refineries' violence.

7
Institute for Policy Studies

Before there was a geographic place or a legal entity known as The Institute for Policy Studies, there was a group of people who met, planned, argued, concerted, and acted as if the Institute already existed. The first Institute project appeared on the wings of a worldwide crisis that threatened nuclear genocide between the United States and the Soviet Union.

I woke up on a Sunday morning in October, 1962 to an ominous lead story in the *Washington Post*. It said something weird was going on. Kennedy Administration officials who had been scattered around the country, campaigning toward a general election just a few weeks later, had been disappearing, only to reappear in secrecy in Washington, DC. Nobody knew why. It felt like a crisis, but nobody knew what it was.

I knew Karl Meyer, the reporter who wrote the story. I called him midday. He said he'd been able to confirm that the subject was Cuba, but nothing more. His Monday article would report that much.

Then I began calling my peacenik friends. It was UN Week, the anniversary of the United Nation's founding. Many of them were away from DC too, speaking to pro-UN audiences. I told them something big was happening involving foreign policy and Cuba. They should come back to Washington.

Meyer's story appeared on Monday morning. It had little more than he'd told me, but just enough that some officials began adding more meat to the story. President Kennedy decided to speak to the nation on Monday night, a day or two earlier than he had originally intended. So a bunch of us who had been imagining the Institute met in a hotel room: Leo Szilard, "inventor" of the atomic bomb, who together with Albert Einstein had written President Franklin Delano Roosevelt the fateful letter urging the U.S. start work making the bomb.

Who else was involved in that pre-IPS group? Marc Raskin and Dick Barnet, at that point both officials inside the U.S. government, trying to create a policy that would make such a crisis impossible. Don Michael and I, at that point research fellows for a tiny Peace Research Institute.

Gar Alperovitz, author of a book that used deep research in diplomatic archives to show that the atomic-bombing of Hiroshima and Nagasaki were aimed not at defeating Japan but at intimidating the Soviet Union.

Kennedy explained that Soviet ships bearing nuclear missiles were on the high seas, taking the missiles to Cuba. He said they must not land since those missiles would be a threat to the lives of all Americans. He declared a blockade, forcing Soviet ships to turn back even if that led to war. He said that "Victory would be ashes in our mouths." I remember grinding my teeth and muttering, "Our mouths will be ashes in our mouths." Kennedy did not mention that there were U.S. nuclear missiles on high alert in Turkey, as close to the Soviet heartland as these Soviet missiles would be to the American heartland, already endangering "them" as Kennedy feared their missiles would endanger "us."

That Monday night, the pre-Institute group met in Leo Szilard's hotel apartment to watch Kennedy explain what was happening. Two of us, Barnet and Raskin, were actually in the administration. Barnet worked for the Arms Control and Disarmament Agency, and Raskin in the National Security Council—and they knew what all this meant. They understood what it meant to *risk* a nuclear war—rather, "exchange"—"responsible officials" didn't use words like "war," "holocaust," that might scare people! A nuclear *exchange* with the Soviet Union. They understood what it meant to do that. The rest of us did too. For example, I'd been doing research on nuclear disarmament and nuclear deterrence and the bomb and so on, for about two years, and had written a book already about it.

So we were absorbing what this meant, and trying to figure out what to do to save our lives, literally our lives, and who knew, fifty, seventy-five, a hundred million other people. We started trying to figure out what these two crazy people—that is, Kennedy and Khruschev—needed. We thought, there might be a way for them to save face, if a third person could somehow glow with enough magic to get them to back off long enough to be able to catch their breath and the whole world to catch its breath. Who could do such a thing? Not the UN, because it is made up of just more of the same governmental leaders. No magic.

John XXIII was Pope. He was a peacenik, he was a *mensch*. At that point, no Pope had ever been out of Europe. We figured that if he flew to New York, to the UN, and asked Kennedy and Khruschev to meet him at the UN, there might be enough magic. They might be able to do it. So the question became, "Who's going to ask the Pope?"

Well, Leo Szilard, who invented the atomic bomb, was sitting in the room. "Leo, you call the Pope."

Leo says, "Me? I am an old man. I always have my suitcase packed, two hundred dollars, and my passport. And tomorrow morning, I am flying to Geneva."

He said, "If the crisis gets any further than where it is right now, the European countries will proclaim their neutrality—they think the United States is crazy anyway—and the only place it will be reasonably safe is Europe. At Geneva, my pals are at the European Center for Nuclear Research."

He then turned to Marc Raskin and asked him if he wanted to send his daughter Erika to Geneva. "Thanks, but no," said Marc.

Szilard added, "You are young all of you, so you call the Pope."

"Leo, if you call the Pope, he *will* answer the phone."

"I'm an old man, I'm going to Geneva with my passport in hand. Forget it." He had *just*—literally, he had just—founded an organization called the Council for Abolishing War, which later changed its name to the Council for a Livable World. So we said, "But you're—the Council for Abolishing War!"

Then the phone in his apartment began to ring. The people all over the country who had sent money in to become members.

"I don't have any advice. I'm leaving tomorrow morning," Szilard was saying.

So the rest of us started talking. "All right, what can we do?" One of us knew a guy who had studied with Martin Buber, who was still alive. Would Buber call the Pope? We figured Martin Buber could reach the Pope, and his student could reach Martin Buber.

This was networking, but at a very intense level, in a very intense moment. And the people who were the main actors, we couldn't reach: I mean, the Kennedy White House sealed off the Secretary of State, the Secretary of Defense, Bobby Kennedy. They were sealed off. There was no way you could lobby them. Normally, a senator would have called the White House and said "What are you *doing*?" But there was no way to do it.

When I got home that night, I explained to my wife what we had been doing about saving the world, including the Buber thing. She looked at me and said, "What do you think? Buber, Mr. I-Thou, he's going to call *God*, and *God* is going to call the Pope?"

We had several other avenues that we were hoping would get to the Pope. One of us knew that the papal legate to the U.S. was meeting that week with Norman Cousins, president of the National Committee for a Sane Nuclear Policy. In fact, it turned out, the Pope was at work on an encyclical called *Pacem in Terris,* the first papal encyclical in history directed not to the Church but to all humanity. It was issued the next Easter, about the bomb, an extraordinary document, almost certainly affected by the missile crisis.

Meanwhile, SDS (Students for a Democratic Society) was on its way to demonstrate in Washington, just to do it. As Raskin said, the only thing we could really do in this situation was preserve the First Amendment. And there was nothing we could do about whether there was going to be nuclear desolation or not. If it comes, it comes.

That was the week when nobody in the city of Washington smiled. I mean that truly. Because, pretty much all of us expected to die. But we didn't. It has all remained for me a complex lesson in ineffectiveness, effectiveness. I mean, being effective in simply keeping yourself awake and committed. The effectiveness of *not* surrendering, *not* giving up, even though it seemed impossible to have any effect on the body politic. But keeping ourselves committed to what we believed in—except for Leo Szilard, which was also a lesson—I mean, that was also a powerful lesson.

None of us at that time would have evoked the Spirit, but in retrospect it was the Spirit of love and liberation that called us into action when there was no "practical" way to make a difference. During that week, Marcus as national-security staff to the White House was offered a place in the well-stocked, well-cemented hiding-place in the West Virginia mountains. He said, "What about my wife and my daughter Erika?" He was told, "That would be nepotism." But from another way of thinking about the world, that would be not love, but nepotism. Marc said, "Thanks, but no thanks."

In fact, that week is what led Barnet and Raskin to leave government and begin working to create the Institute. They began seriously imagining it then, bringing together a bunch of smart and effective people. They decided the government was crazy, that there was no more to do inside it.

* * *

The first deep experience I had that religious commitment, even ecstasy, could be fused with political change came from Rev. Charles Sherrod. He was an activist, religiously passionate, beloved by the Spirit. Sherrod was a SNCC (Student Nonviolent Coordinating

Committee) organizer who carried his organizing into his religious life in southwest Georgia—the town of "All-benny," to spell it the way he pronounced it.

Already by 1963 the Institute had become a place of restful recovery for temporarily burnt-out SNCC workers. They suffered from physical and emotional trauma as they faced police dogs, prison terms, and KKK murderers as they worked for equality in drugstores and voting booths.

One day the Institute announced a seminar on the civil rights movement to be led by Sherrod from Albany. We invited friendly members of Congress. A dozen came.

Sherrod began in the quiet tones of a college professor teaching a political science seminar. Slowly his voice modulated into the melody of a Black preacher in his church on Sunday morning—gently inviting "the Lord" to protect his people, crashing into thunder as he spoke of torture in the prisons, of dogs set on children in the streets. Subsiding to a whisper drenched with unshed tears. I had never heard anything like it. Neither had the Congressmembers. I never forgot it.

* * *

The second trickle of suggestion that the Spirit and social transformation belonged clasped in unity came in 1964 in the Atlantic City convention of the Democratic Party. The Mississippi Freedom Democratic Party's racially integrated delegation challenged the all-white pro-segregation delegation to be recognized as the true representatives of Mississippi to the national Democratic Party. The Freedom Democrats had been elected in unofficial balloting at Black churches in Mississippi, because Black citizens were beaten or killed if they tried to register to vote in the official elections.

Marc Raskin and I were invited to support the Freedom Democrats, even though we were outsiders to the Party. Why us? Because as former legislative assistants on Capitol Hill, we had gotten to know some of the Congressmembers who were members of the credentials committee of the convention. We might be able to invite them to talk with Dr. Martin Luther King, who could tell them what Mississippi was really like. He himself had also been invited by the Freedom Democrats, though he was to some degree an outsider to its struggle.

For me, that night was the most impressive experience of Dr. King. More than the great charismatic speeches. That night, he wasn't charismatic at all. He had a badly twisted ankle, was walking with crutches. He was working hard, sweating at 112 degrees in an un-air-conditioned room at Atlantic City's Convention Hall. His job was to convince hard-bitten politicians who feared President Lyndon Johnson's power, to brave his wrath. He explained, over and over, what Mississippi was really like for Black folk. And he persuaded ten members of the credentials committee—the minimum required to bring a minority report to the floor for a full public prime-time debate on seating the Freedom Democrats. Triumph!

But not quite. President Johnson quickly offered a compromise. Two members of the Freedom Party would be chosen to sit in the Mississippi seats. The all-white delegation would be seated only if they promised in advance to support the convention's nominees in the general election—expected to be Johnson for president and Hubert Humphrey of Minnesota, a supporter of civil rights, for vice-president. Then there were rumors that if the liberals kept supporting the Freedom Democrats, Johnson would dump Humphrey. Some of the liberals had always expected the MFDP could win only a symbolic victory, and here—they had it—two seats. Under threat and "promise," the liberal edge of the pro-Freedom Democrats' coalition began to buckle.

Someone asked, who gets to choose the two MFDP delegates to be seated? An answer came: The President! The President? Not the Party itself? No. Johnson was not about to hear Fannie Lou Hamer get to speak on TV to the whole American people in prime time. After all, her body, badly beaten when she showed up to register, was already as eloquent as her tongue.

The Freedom Democrats were uninterested. Ms. Hamer spoke

the truth, refusing to make it an issue of herself: "We didn't come here for no two seats when ALL of us is tired!"

Next evening, when the Convention gathered, the Oregon delegates turned their tickets and badges over to the Freedom Democrats, who took the Mississippi seats. The convention police came to "restore order" and expel them. I was one of the "outsiders" who stood in the way. "Please move, sir. We need to restore order, sir!" "I'm trying to move, officer, but I can't. The aisle is jammed with people. Nobody's budging."

"Sir, I said MOVE!" "I'm trying!" Then I moved an inch, then slithered back an inch. "See how hard it is, officer?"

It took forty minutes to remove Black Mississippi from their seats.

The following day, Ms. Hamer led us all onto the Atlantic City Boardwalk, to sing and carry picket signs. One song pierced my half-forgotten Jewish soul. First time I ever heard a Passover song in a Black trope, a Black melody:

> Go tell it on the mountain,
> Over the hills and everywhere—
> Go tell it on the mountain,
> Let my people go!
>
> Who are the people dressed in black,
> Let my people go-oh,
> Must be the hypocrites a-turnin' back;
> Let my people go-oh!
>
> Who are the people dressed in red?
> Let my people go-oh,
> Must be the people [and I readied myself to hear
> "that Moses led!"—but it came out different] Bob
> Moses led!
> Let my people go-oh!

Oh my God, I said to myself. Bob Moses was one of the bravest, most far-sighted, of the SNCC workers who had helped organize alongside Ms. Hamer. Bob Moses, who spent time in Parchman, the foulest of Mississippi's prisons. Ms. Hamer had not only made Passover a Black moment through a Black song, she had summoned the 3,000-year-old tradition to appear right then. Right now! "Bob Moses," of course!

That went into my soul like a seed to grow. Spirit and social transformation unified. The walls of millennia crashing down, the wall between Spirit and the people crashing down. Not the wall between church and state, which the Constitution protects, but the wall between the Spirit and the People.

* * *

Marc Raskin and I were both part-time legislative assistants in the fall of 1959 in the office of freshman Congressman Robert W. Kastenmeier of Wisconsin. Marc grew up in Milwaukee, discovered he was a child prodigy at piano, studied at Juilliard under Rosina Lhevinne, and finished a law degree at the University of Chicago. Drawn toward both politics and piano, he found his brain even more nimble than his fingers—and came to live in Washington and make creative political change.

At Congressman Kastenmeier's request, Marc and I worked together on uncovering the bio-war preparations of the U.S. military at Fort Detrick: anthrax, bubonic/pneumonic plague, psittacosis. When we had enough information to show that the Chemical Corps was lying about its "non-lethal" arsenal, I prepared and sent out a press release with the facts.

But I made a mistake in arithmetic. The press release counted up more civilian illnesses resulting from this germ-war research than was actually the case.

I discovered the error before the press did and went—horrified at the damage it might do the Congressman and the work, and terrified at having blundered in my first important task—to tell Marc what I'd done. What should I do?

"Three things," he said. "Tell Bob right now. Put out a correction before the press can nail us. And remember: today's newspaper is used to wrap fish tomorrow." (This was long before the internet.)

The content was correct and wise, but the tone of his advice was even wiser: It was loving, rueful but comforting.

Marc taught me to be *chutzpadik* (courageous/nervey) without being arrogant. In the summer of 1960, with the Congressman back home campaigning and little for us to do in Washington, he said one day: "We have time on our hands. Let's find out what 'deterrence' really means. All these generals talk about it, but they never say how it's supposed to work." So we called the Pentagon and arranged to interview the leading experts of the Army, Navy, Air Force, and Office of the Secretary of Defense about deterrence. They had names straight from a morality play: Admiral Ward, General Spear, and so on.

They all had different versions of deterrence. And we soon realized that each was right—about the others. The Air Force showed the Navy's version was crazy; the Navy showed the Air Force version was crazy; and they all proved that the Office of the Secretary of Defense, which tried to mix all the versions together in order to please every branch of the military, was craziest of all. We wrote what began as a report to our own congressman. It then became a report to all of Congress that stirred the Air Force to pay a publicity firm millions to refute it, and then our paper became a book.

We wrote together in a rhythm: We talked about each chapter in depth, then I drafted a version, we talked again, Marc marked revisions in the margin, I revised the text, and so on till we were both satisfied.

Why do I call this *chutzpadik*? I'd thought I was not allowed to write such a book before I finished my PhD. Before I'd spent years studying military strategy. Before I'd gained credentials and a reputation. What Marc was showing me was that, precisely because we were outsiders, uncredentialled, we could see the emperor's nakedness. It was *chutzpah* without power, without the arrogance born of power, that could reveal the truth.

Along the way, I realized that as we wrote, Marc was teaching something profound without ever quite saying it. He was pushing me, us, to go deeper into the issues, philosophically deeper: Why were the different theories, coming from such practical men of war, so impractical and crazy? Why did the Air Force line on deterrence switch so flagrantly from "Target cities to deter all nuclear war; nobody can win one" to "Targeting cities is immoral; target the enemy's missile sites and strike first to prevail." And why did the Navy's line switch in exactly the other direction?

Why did these generals keep talking about "games"? Why did they use sexual language like "wargasm" and "protecting the CONUS [Continental U.S.]?"

Always, Marc kept pushing for the why beneath the what. He taught me that good politics was rooted in serious philosophy. In the process, I became far more deeply focused and even—I wryly realized—more intelligent than I had been as a slightly maverick but mostly unexceptional grad student.

Over the next several years, Marcus drew together intellectuals like Paul Goodman, Jim Warburg, Leo Szilard, and David Riesman with a batch of Members of Congress. Marc called this amalgam "the American neurosis": Each group was astonished to be paid attention by the other. Joe DiMaggio marveled that he got to marry the sexiest woman in America; Marilyn Monroe marveled that she got to marry the greatest sports star in the world. Marc used this "neurosis to bring together scholars who were enraptured by their first conversations with Congressfolk, with Congressfolk who were enchanted by their first conversations with famous scholars." He called this amalgam the Liberal Project, and, in this way, defined a non-Cold War version of what might be called participatory liberalism. It opened up much of the intellectual space that made possible liberal opposition to the U.S. war against Vietnam and liberal empathy with the emerging New Left.

Then for two years, Marc worked inside the Kennedy Administration, on the staff of the National Security Council, resisting every step of the way as McGeorge Bundy dragged it down the road to hell: the Vietnam War. Bundy tried to force Marc to scuttle the book on deterrence that he and I had written together, as the price of Marc's keeping his job.

Marc asked David Riesman and Erich Fromm to meet with us to work out what to do. He insisted that scuttling the book was unacceptable, off the table. We brought our wives to the meeting, thinking they had a big stake in what happened—but Fromm and Riesman shooed them out, muttering that women's emotions had no place in this matter. I was astounded—this from two leading proponents of love as a social imperative? But then I was even more astounded by Fromm's contemptuous attitude toward Riesman. Afterward, I asked Marc why, and he explained that Fromm had been Riesman's personal psychoanalyst. For me, that contradicted what therapy should be. Maybe Marc was just being sarcastic—he occasionally commented on the world that way.

I could feel the Spirit rapidly falling. But the four of us finally agreed to take Marc's name off the book (*The Limits of Defense*, Doubleday, 1962) but adamantly refused to halt its publication. Fromm and Riesman agreed that to boost the book's prestige against losing Marc's name, one of them would write a preface, and the other, a blurb for the back cover.

Bundy backed down. Marc kept his job. My name remained. The two famous people kept their promises of support.

Marc kept his own integrity and independence by making sure he had a peer group outside the government, whom he trusted to tell him honestly when they thought he was being coopted by the government's assumptions and priorities.

As a result, there were odd scenes: At first, a visitor got to see Marc (or anybody else in the Executive Office Building) by walking in the front door, taking the elevator, and knocking on the door to Marc's office. Then President Kennedy hired General Maxwell Taylor to be his military expert. Taylor started demanding credentials checks at the front door and each elevator stop. Bundy had to prove he was just as important as Taylor, so he ordered the same credentials checks.

I once bumped into Paul Goodman, the famous anarchist author. He would refuse to obey the law and take cover when civil defense alarms went off. "Taking cover will protect me from an atomic bomb?" he laughed. Entering to visit Marc, as I was leaving, Goodman was detained at the elevator, to produce some ID. "ID? I know who I am, I don't carry my name in my pocket!" he said. In despair, the desk officer called Marc's office. Marc said—"Oh God! Yeah, that sounds exactly like Goodman. Send him up already." When the desk officer said Goodman could pass, he objected: "But how do you know I am who I say I am?" he said, hitching up the rope he used for a belt.

And there was the time when Marc arranged for Ralph Ellison, the brilliant Black writer, to take part in a White House discussion on education. Afterwards, people gathered to unwind and schmooze at Marc and Barbara's house. "I got this letter from—from THE WHITE HOUSE!" laughed Ellison. I thought THE WHITE HOUSE wanted me—and it turned out to be a Jewish leprechaun!"

When Kennedy came close to blowing up the world in the Cuban Missile Crisis, Raskin and Richard Barnet, a disarmament advocate at the Arms Control and Disarmament Agency, decided that internal resistance was no longer useful, that an outside voice needed to be created. So by 1963, Marcus, working with Barnet and a group of other young intellectuals including Gar Alperovitz, Christopher Jencks, Milton Kotler, Donald Michael, and me, founded the Institute for Policy Studies: a center for action and research that would have connections inside the Federal government but would not depend on it for money or legitimacy. That as outsiders we could be chutzpadik without arrogance.

Through the '60s, we worked not only against the Vietnam War and the arms race but for grassroots neighborhood democracy, for new approaches to the media that would make them mass enlighteners instead of mass mind-polluters, for a democratic healthcare system, for the empowerment of Black communities.

Early in 1968, Marc was indicted and tried along with Dr. Benjamin Spock, Rev. William Sloane Coffin, and others for conspiring to aid and abet resistance to the draft. The general case against Marc would have been reasonably accurate if it had focused solely on the Call to Resist Illegitimate Authority.

What was that? One morning in 1967, drawing on his favorite philosophic wellspring for action, Marc said to me, "What would Sartre do about this war against Vietnam?" I said, "He would have written a manifesto for other writers to join. He would have focused on the individual moral and ethical choice facing young men about the military draft. Then he would have gotten it published as widely as possible." "I agree—good Sartre!" he said. "Let's do it!"

So we wrote it—our "Call to Resist." We strengthened each other's work as we had back in 1960, with what became *The Limits of Defense*. We sent it to the *New York Review of Books*, which published it and sent it sailing in the wide wide world, gathering thousands of signatures from campuses and houses of worship.

It was the "Call to Resist" that got Marc and me invited to join an anti-war delegation that met with an assistant attorney general inside the Department of Justice. We had a briefcase filled with 1,000 draft cards (illegally, according to that same department), turned over to antiwar activists, instead of being dutifully carried by the draft-prone young men assigned to kill and die in Vietnam.

I remember only two incidents from that meeting: The first one of us to speak was a young Black man from Berkeley. He fixed the assistant attorney general with a steady gaze until the room grew utterly quiet and the official looked back at him. Then he said: "You don't exist. You are the imaginary ghost of a destructive machine. I am alive and real; I have nothing to say to you." And he walked out.

Long silence from all of us.

The second incident that I remember began when one of us

presented the briefcase and its thousand draft cards to the official, explaining what was in it and why. He said fiercely, "I will not receive this. Take it away!" I banged my hand on the briefcase and said, "You in this department claim this is evidence of an illegal act—refusing to carry a draft card. You are a high law-enforcement official. Yet you choose to ignore evidence of what you claim is a crime." Soon after that, we all left, with the guilty briefcase sitting on the table. As we left, a dozen FBI agents who had been waiting outside the room rushed in. They grabbed the briefcase.

If the FBI and DOJ had stuck to the "Call to Resist" they might have had a winning case against Marc and me. But they seemed to be mesmerized by the briefcase with 1,000 draft cards. Even worse, they somehow got convinced that Marc, not I, had pounded on that briefcase. So their facts were false, and the case against Marc was by far the flimsiest.

I remember especially one moment on the very day of the indictments. An Institute student had, a week before, asked Marc to write a letter of recommendation for some future post. After the announcement, after the hordes of press had departed, the student turned to Marc and said: "I guess that now you're charged with a crime I shouldn't have you write that letter."

Marc wheeled. His face flashed. "Oh yes you will!" he said. "No bad faith. We stand together. If you wanted me a week ago, you want me now."

The student paled. "Yes, of course. You're right." That existential flash of clarity and courage, over and over repeated, was for me the most powerful teaching I took from Marc.

There were some arenas of my life and thought that he did not nourish. For example, for him and for the rest of the Institute leadership, it took many years to hear the voices of justice and of creativity in feminism. And he was mostly just intrigued, rarely hostile, responding to my journey into a progressive religious path and Jewish renewal. My role at IPS gave me the time and freedom in 1968-69 to write *The Freedom Seder* and to take a vigorous part in my emerging Jewish life. And it was Marc's advice to the editors of *Ramparts* magazine that brought them to publish *The Freedom Seder* in early 1969, giving it its national audience and constituency.

Yet the more I pursued the creation of a justice-committed Judaism with the *havurah* or fellowship movement as a field of work, the less the Institute seemed pleased. I remember a moment when Marc asked me to substitute for him in a meeting. I told him I couldn't; there was a Talmud study group I needed to be at. "Talmud?" he said in a tone of disbelief. I could hear unspoken something like, *I admire your focus on the Torah of justice. The Torah is a great document of western civilization. But* Talmud—*obscurantist, obsessive!*

I responded, "Marc, three members of the Talmud study group are also members of the executive committee of Breira, the organization that has been fighting for Israel to end its occupation of Palestinian territories in favor of an independent Palestine living in peace alongside Israel." He simply repeated, "Talmud?" in a sorrowful tone. So maybe that was at the root of my leaving IPS, which I finally did in 1977.

For me, that path was one in which, as he had taught, I kept peeling away the layers of fact to explore the deeper truths from which they had grown. And I brought to religious thought and practice the sense of an outsider's chutzpah to question and to see those deeper truths.

Marc wrote some works of broad synthesis—especially *Being and Doing* (1971). His work infused the thought of a great number of the independent-minded radicals of the past fifty years. Yet, his most enduring work, in my opinion, was bringing together in the Institute for Policy Studies other extraordinary people—and people who became extraordinary as he helped them ask themselves the "Why?" He nourished within each of us the spark of progressive creativity and the courage to act when the moment demands it. It was a place to stand together, a place where thought and action could fuse into what Marc called "not cold facts, but hot facts."

I was deeply saddened to hear of Marc's death in 2017. From

1959 to 1975, he was my friend, teacher, student, co-author, co-activist, and hero, even when we bitterly disagreed.

Just three years earlier, in 2014 when Marc turned eighty, I wanted to send him a gift and remembered his playing the piano. I knew he'd been a child prodigy, that he quit regular school to study at Juilliard, and after studying piano for a year in Italy he organized a recital at Carnegie Hall, which the critics didn't appreciate. For all I knew, they might have dissed him because he was as far ahead in piano as he was in politics. Either way, he decided to play the black and white keys of a great social movement, rather than the musical instrument. So, I sent Marc a batch of tapes—classical piano played by great pianists and modern post-classical piano music played by fine pianists. He responded with a joyful and enthusiastic phone call. *Thank God!* I thought. *The Spirit has risen from great depths.* "Sheh'hekhianu! Praised be the One who fills us with life!" I am glad we both lived long enough for me to be able to say this aloud to him.

***

Congress passed a special tax on telephone service to pay for the U.S. war in Vietnam. My then-wife, Irene, and I decided to refuse to pay it.

The telephone company was not interested in enforcing the tax. For years, it reported non-payment to the U.S. government, but continued to supply our phone service. Then, finally, a phone call came from the Internal Revenue Service. "We understand you have not been paying your phone tax." "That's right." (Don't lie to the gummint. That's a separate crime, often much more serious. Truth or silence, that's the ticket.)

"Umm, we'd like to meet with you, talk with you." "OK. I suggest my workplace, the Institute for Policy Studies."

"Umm. Are you sure, sir?" (Hardly anybody wants their boss to know they are not paying their taxes.) "Yes, that's fine." "OK then." And we set a date.

Next day, I sent around IPS a memo that there will be a seminar on the ethics of tax refusal. Leaders: two IRS agents and me. Open to all, including a limited number of friends and colleagues from outside IPS.

When the IRS showed up, one was an ex-Marine, tough and bossy; the other, thin and quiet, Black former high-school teacher. Aha, bad cop/good cop. Bad cop starts, "What you are doing is illegal, you are in serious trouble, but if you pay up, we can probably smooth it out. *Probably* (with a scowl), if you are quick!" Good cop: "Look. I agree with you about the war, it's really terrible, but this is a democracy, nobody can just take the law into their own hands, that's why we have elections. Get Congress to repeal the tax and end the war, bring all our boys home, nobody wants all these wonderful young guys killed."

I responded with a combination of individual conscience and social justice, and then a bit about the post-World War II Nuremberg court decision that citizens of a country violating laws of humanity are legally responsible to take action to stop the government violations. I closed with urging the two IRS cops to resign their jobs. It was a good seminar.

※ ※ ※

Early in 1975, the Fellows of the Institute were told that for financial reasons the Institute would continue to pay only half salary and the other half would have to be raised by the fellows themselves. We were stunned. There had been no consultation, no bringing together of the fellows to discuss an Institute-wide financial problem, no discussion of how to solve it. Simply a decree.

For me and for many of us, this violated a basic agreement when we had started in 1963. I remember Marc Raskin saying he wished he could use the title "rector" instead of "director," because it encouraged us, as in English university practice, to be more egalitarian among all the fellows. But he and his co-director, Dick Barnet, concluded that "rector" was too strange a label for the American scene. So for twelve years, they had been co-directors. During that time, there had been only one challenge to their power to make important decisions. That was when a number of the fellows realized that we were all male and we could not continue to violate one of the increasingly powerful commitments of progressive organizations.

At that point, Marc and Dick were not feminists and had no interest in breaking the Institute's conventions to bring a woman as a resident fellow. According to the rules, the two of them had veto power over visiting fellows and associate fellows. But for some strange quirk of the bylaws, their veto did not apply to resident fellows.

There were a few resident fellows who rarely showed up. They had other jobs and were not on the Institute payroll. But they still had the title. They were Black and had become connected with the Institute as it worked closely with SNCC. So those of us who were on the scene and felt strongly about one associate fellow, Charlotte Bunch, persuaded one of the Black residents to come to a meeting to elect Bunch a resident. He did, and it worked. Marc and Dick were dismayed—I think far more for the afront to their power than for the specifics of naming Bunch.

The decree about half salaries came a few months later. And for me, there were philosophical, emotional, and practical reasons to be upset by it. One was its violation of the principle of equality. The second was my close friendship with Marc, which now felt cast in deep doubt. The third was my kids, one of them eleven years old, the other eight. The constituency I had been working with since 1969 and *The Freedom Seder* were lower- and middle-income Jews, not the rich. So the new decree felt like a practical attack on my ability to care for my family, as well as an attack on equality at the Institute, and an attack on the hope of a democratic transformation of American Jewry.

Other fellows had different but similar practical and philosophical objections. So we did the unheard of. We formed a union at a progressive organization. It was peculiar because we had at least as much commitment to do our work as management of the Institute had, and so the threat of a strike seemed meaningless. Meanwhile, my close friendship with Marc was in peril: "You promised to be rectors, egalitarians among the fellows. This doesn't feel very egalitarian."

Things got so bitter inside the Institute that Mark and Dick invited an outsider to figure out a solution. He came up with another plan: Any fellow who wished to leave would receive a departure allowance based on how long they had spent at the Institute. That was less than half a salary, but at least it left us with our dignity as free scholar-activists. And it gave us the challenge of creating a new institution that would embody our values more effectively.

I chose to leave.

* * *

We set up a new group, the Public Resource Center. We met with each other to exchange ideas much more than had become our habit at the Institute.

One creative purr from the Spirit took place when I asked a colleague, the renowned radical journalist Jim Ridgeway, if he had any recommendations for how to advance my Jewish-renewal organizing. He said, "What I did was start a periodic newsletter to reach my folks. You might try that." So I did. And to my astonishment, a mailing brought in 4,000 subscribers for *Menorah: Sparks of Jewish Renewal*. It was the first time that label for our movement had been used nationally. Reb Zalman liked it, and it was adopted by his B'nai Or folks. I loved gathering articles on new liturgy and new graphics; I loved being publisher, editor, and schlepper of bundles to the post office for each issue. The Spirit smiled.

Then, one of our previous Institute colleagues, Leonard Rodberg, who held a Ph.D. in physics and had been working to keep the hospital system of New York City non-profit, rather than corporate, shared something going on in the Jimmy Carter administration in D.C.

Leonard and I shared a political outlook, and a concern to apply that outlook to American energy businesses, which were central to the American economy and society. As a physicist, he knew something I didn't—that any energy system built on burning coal and oil was more and more swiftly overheating planet Earth. He knew there was a small group of people in the Carter administration who'd begun to worry about this. That was why Carter put solar collectors on the roof of the White House. That was why Carter appointed a small group of progressives from Washington to a community-oriented division of the Department of Energy.

So Leonard and I went to those folks in the Department of Energy with a proposal that they grant us enough money to do a preliminary study of whether there might be enough support in Washington for a solar-energy coop. We got the grant. We did the study. There clearly was some energy in DC that wanted help in creating their own solar-energy coop. We wrote up the results and submitted them.

Our sponsors were happy and suggested we take the next step. So we developed a whole project proposal for actually organizing a solar-energy coop in DC. Our friends applauded, offered us a contract to do that work and we agreed. I remember that in my own first draft, both the timing and the language of the solar-energy coop and campaign centered around the Jewish festival of Sukkot. One crucial member of the energy department team was Rev. Channing Phillips with whom I had been close friends while he was the chair of the Democratic delegates to the Democratic National Convention in Chicago. (You may recall that after we picked Robert F. Kennedy as our candidate for President, and he was murdered, we named our chair, Rev. Phillips, as our candidate. So he and I had a bond.) He liked the Sukkot proposal.

But he came back to us half laughing and half groaning. He said, we showed it to our lawyers, and they said "Are you crazy? Have you never heard of the First Amendment, preventing the federal government from supporting a religious congregation or festival?" So we re-wrote the proposal without Sukkot, and this time it passed muster with strong support.

We were ready to go ahead. Then in November 1980, Jimmy Carter lost re-election. Ronald Reagan took over the government. He took the solar collectors off the White House roof and nobody in his newly appointed Department of Energy was interested in solar energy. Or, for that matter, any kind of coop that would be ruled according to one person, one vote, rather than one dollar, one vote.

So there we were, a pittance for a salary and nowhere to take the vision that was drawing me ever more powerfully: building a Jewish community on *havurot*, small egalitarian prayer communities. It was then that I came up with the idea of a book on the Jewish holidays, *Seasons of Our Joy*. I had the publisher pay the advance money to the Public Resource Center, and used it to pay me a salary. When it ran out, I applied for unemployment compensation.

That carried me into early 1982. My brother Howard suggested I turn the basement of our house into an independent apartment, so that the rent could help support me. My father lent me the money to redo the basement, but otherwise, I felt bereft. Emotionally stranded from my closest friend, Marc Raskin. Financially stranded from— well, everywhere. And stranded from creative Judaism, because there was no institution in Washington able to support, with a salary, fresh ideas for the Jewish world. Jews for Urban Justice—activists—had very little money.

* * *

My beloved rabbi and life partner, Phyllis Berman, teaches that the aspect of God often called *Gevurah*, which many people call outward defense, should best be reframed as the form love takes when directed inward toward one's self. It is this kind of self-acceptance, love for self, that does not degenerate into egotism, but connects with others, that generates *chesed*—love for others.

It is not always easy to live with this aspect of Spirit. As I write these encounters, I find rising within me the desire to re-feel, more than rethink, my relationship with Marc Raskin. Much of this exploration arose because I kept stumbling over the long separation between my close friend and me.

It was not just that I was trying to come to terms, sixty years later, with my separation from the Institute for Policy Studies. It was much more, the scene inextricably tangled with the break-up of what I thought was a lifelong friendship. For a moment I will jump over the breakup and its long silence, for what it was like to reestablish connection after the long silence. Marc gave it a name on a visit that Phyllis and I had with him at a time of his physical and intellectual decline. Responding to something I said, he remarked, full of surprise, "A soft Arthur Waskow!"

I had never thought of myself as hard or harsh but it was clear that Marc did. My relationship to him and to the Institute had been based on a tough commitment to justice and its rule. Looking back at the breakup, I can hear that underneath was his own sense of broken friendship. He was not very adept at communicating that—more like radiating it than like saying it—and only now, years later, could I hear it.

When he said he thought maybe I was being dragged into opposition by wild horses, I think now he was saying that we had been so close that it would take cavalry to tear us apart. That's what I felt too. But I never got even as close as he did to saying so. And there were dozens of small explosions that make sense to me in retrospect only, as sorrow manifesting as anger. Once in the midst of the Great Rebellion, I asked for his advice about where to go and what to do as I left the Institute. He suggested I explore a Washington think tank that was ultra-right wing. He knew that I knew that place with horror, and he knew that I knew they would see me as anathema.

Another time, a few years after the breakup, and with another leader of the Institute sitting with us listening, he suddenly went into a rage because the new think-and-act center we had formed had accepted money from the federal government. His rage made no "rational" sense. We were no longer the Institute that had pledged not to do this. The federal agency that provided the money was really a group of Washington progressives acting on their own with a very small dish of federal largesse, but it was clear that he was still bitter. It was also clear that his bitterness was rooted, just as mine had been, in our deeply shared commitment to "rules" that embodied our inner hearing for our inner selves. For me: the rule of equality among the fellows. For him: the rules about no money from the Feds.

Another time, he mentioned that it was hard to think about an Institute without me. I cut across the thought by saying the Jewish community would never understand if I returned to IPS, but I realize now he was trying to say that he missed me, and it was I who turned it into a rule. My whole face wrinkles up to hold back tears as I say this.

There are two moments that I am proudest of in those years of awkwardly trying to reestablish ties. One is that twenty years after leaving IPS I brought a large delegation of elders –veterans of the Black-led American movement to fulfill democracy that most people call the Civil Rights Movement. I brought about a dozen elders to Washington to visit the memorial statue for Dr. King, and then to come to IPS where there had been so much energy to assist the Black-led movement.

I glanced up just as Marc walked into the room. I used my voice to gather up everyone who was there and said: "In some parts of my ancient Jewish tradition, there is the idea that students should stand when their teacher walks into the room. I've never been a fan of that idea, because I think that the best of Jewish process is the notion that teacher and student are really intertwined." But my teacher of decades had just walked into the room, and I explained to the crowd I had stood to recognize and honor him.

It has been very strange and a welcoming of Spirit in a guise I never expected, for me to look inward and find the Spirit wearing the costume of a soft Arthur Waskow. Maybe it took my own aging to remember that Marc told me years and years ago that he was blind in one eye and that I never said a word of sadness or comfort. That was the hard part of Arthur acting as if only armor could protect us radicals against the world. I am glad I lived long enough to begin to find a softer me. I am sorry he did not live long enough for us to befriend each other anew in the joys of "soft."

8

1968: The Longest Year

For me, the story of the Chicago Democratic Convention of 1968 begins early in 1968, in the auditorium of a dilapidated old public school in the Adams-Morgan neighborhood of Washington City, DC.

In many of the city's neighborhoods, simmering bubbles of bitterness about its treatment of Black citizens and simmering opposition to the war against Vietnam were boiling into anger. Some of us could taste a rebellion coming in July or August. But a nonviolent idea gripped us first: holding neighborhood caucuses to choose people to run as a city-wide slate of candidates. We would seek to become the DC delegation to the Democratic National Convention.

Adams-Morgan, my neighborhood, was one of the very few in Washington that was racially mixed, and it was known as the Movement neighborhood with a strong progressive or even radical bent. So we called a caucus to choose our candidates for the slate to run for the Chicago convention. Around the city, many activists were doing the same in their own neighborhoods. Two of us were elected from Adams-Morgan.

One was Topper Carew, a young Black city planner who was teaching Blacks even younger than himself how to help each other plan a city. He rented a storefront for his teaching. Nobody knew what to call it, so it ended up being called The New Thang. He had shaped what was beginning to be an unplanned newborn political base in the neighborhood, and so he was elected.

I lived in the heart of the neighborhood, and I also had a public presence as a fellow of the Institute for Policy Studies, giving public speeches against the war and for community control of the public schools—which were at that point totally under the control of an appointed commission, an utterly undemocratic process. So I too had an unplanned newborn political base, and I was the other person elected.

Topper and I became good friends. In another neighborhood, a welfare mother was chosen. In still another, a progressive multimillionaire who thought millionaires should be taxed more heavily was chosen. In others, some Democratic Party veterans.

Though our slate was running for a Convention whose main task was to nominate a candidate for president, we had no candidate for president—only a label and a slogan:

"Democrats for Peace and Progress" and "End the War, End Racism, Free DC." We assumed our opponent would be a slate pledged to President Lyndon B. Johnson. We doubted we could win in a city dominated by people Johnson had appointed; yet we thought we could build a strong oppositional base for future action.

On March 16, Senator Robert F. Kennedy announced he was running for president as an antiwar candidate. On Sunday afternoon, March 31, 1968, Johnson announced he would not run for reelection and was sending Averill Harriman, former ambassador to the Soviet Union and former governor of New York, to Paris to negotiate a peace settlement with the Vietnamese.

The nation was astounded. That Sunday afternoon, from all over Washington, antiwar activists went racing to Lafayette Park across from the White House, to dance and sing. I felt a leaden sense of deadness fly up and away as the Spirit rose. I joined in the joyful flyaway to Lafayette Park, and got there just as the gathering was beginning to mutter angrily. The police had just arrested someone for no apparent reason. But then the arrestee reappeared. Brought back by the police because they couldn't conjure up a charge to bring against him! We suddenly felt as if all the cages of government had vanished.

Our ragtag band of insurgents, led by Rev. Channing Phillips, a young Black minister in the MLK mold with grass-roots, nonviolent, antiwar and civil-rights-activist energies, were the leading political force in the city of Washington. Our "Peace and Progress"" slate declared our support for Bobby Kennedy. Then that proved its own snare.

Peter Edelman, a Kennedy aide whom I knew slightly, called me. "I have a message from Ted Sorenson," he said—Bobby's #1 factotum. "He says the senator wants you to drop off the delegate slate. You aren't really a Bobby supporter; you only support him because you think he can end the war. You even wrote that."

I gasped. True enough! But I was my neighborhood's co-nominee. The whole point of our neighborhood caucuses was grass-roots democracy, not a senatorial decree. And some of Bobby's supporters were smitten with him, some with his program. Sorenson might have accepted that argument from a lobbyist for a major corporation—"I'll be loyal to the senator because the corporation named me for the sake of his political program"—but would never have tried to get rid of me if he had cared about democracy for the most interracial, progressive neighborhood in the city. So there was no point in appealing to that argument. Instead I said, "If the senator wants me to drop out, let the senator call and tell me himself." Edelman said, "That's a very good answer." And I never heard another word.

Why was that such a good answer? I'm still not sure. Maybe in the politics of early '68, "honor" and "honesty" were sacred words and notions, even code names for the Spirit rising.

Meanwhile, just four-and-a-half days after a new airiness and lightness seemed to float over America, it came to earth with a heavy crash. On April 4, Martin Luther King, Jr. was murdered with Moses on his lips:

> I've looked over, and I've seen the Promised Land. I may not get there with you. But I want you to know

tonight, that we, as a people, will get to the Promised Land.

Many a Black community in America rose in sorrow, rage, and fire, and many a big city was occupied by its nearest military force in order to control them, the U.S. Army.

* * *

But LBJ still had in him one last rage against those unpatriotic people who thought the Spirit more important than the Law. His last campaign to break us began on January 5, 1968.

The United States announced the indictment of religious, intellectual, and cultural heroes for—the government said—conspiring to disrupt the military draft and the nation's newest war. The defendants said, "Yes! It's the law that's criminal, and the Spirit is just." Best known among the accused were Dr. Benjamin Spock and Rev. William Sloane Coffin, chaplain at Yale, whom we last met in the well-upholstered rooms of the Justice Department. Filling out the list were my good friend Marc Raskin, co-director of IPS; Mitch Goodman, a poet; and Michael Ferber, a Unitarian and a university grad student.

Marc had two immediate tasks: Finding a lawyer, and figuring out what to do with the FBI's one factual mistake: accusing him of banging on that briefcase full of draft cards, when it was actually me. He started his search for a lawyer with the firm that had the Institute for a client: Arnold & Porter. Till recently it had been Arnold, Fortas, & Porter, but Abe Fortas had been transmuted upward when President Johnson appointed him to the Supreme Court. In that way he shone even more luster on the liberal light of the firm, and his wife, Carolyn Agger, a leading tax attorney, was still a partner there.

Surprisingly, Arnold & Porter said no, precipitating an internal battle between its posh partners and its young associates. Why? For weeks the partners didn't talk. But slowly the truth dropped out: A scandal! Johnson had asked Justice Fortas for his advice: Should the

President really have the beloved physician, Dr. Spock, indicted—he who was adored by every mother and grandmother in America? And Justice Fortas responded not by saying, "Lyndon, are you kidding? Are you crazy? The case you'd be creating would be sure to come before the Court! You are setting us both up for a terrible scandal. I'll go home, you go home, this conversation never happened!" Instead, Fortas answered, "Sure you can indict him!"—creating the possible Shakespearean scene for actually such an uproar they both should have known would be unbearable.

So the partners didn't want to take the case, because they knew. Somebody told the young associates. They wanted to take the case, although they knew. And somebody told Marc. So, what to do?

The firm worked out a compromise they offered Marc. The firm would move to sever Marc's case from the others, moving it from Boston to Washington because his only criminal acts were committed right there, in the Department of Justice—banging on that briefcase, remember?—even though that wasn't true. Then with the spotlight off him, they'd quietly drop that case. The government would not object. Peace would break out between the partners and the young associates. Arnold & Porter would fulfill its duty. Marc Raskin would be freed. Everything would be okay.

There was only one problem: Marc said no. He would not sever his case from the rest. No quitting them for an easy dismissal. So Marc still needed a lawyer. The Boston Five were planning a "Nuremberg defense." That is, the trials of the Nazi war criminals at Nuremberg established that citizens of Germany had a positive duty to oppose and resist their government's criminal acts. Just so for American citizens too.

Well, thought Marc, *what lawyer could most effectively present that argument?* The Nuremberg prosecutor, Telford Taylor. He agreed. Next, what about dealing with the weird mistake the FBI had made, naming Marc instead of me as the briefcase-banger? First, Marc should simply tell the truth. Did he do that stuff at that meeting? No. Did anyone? Yes. Did he know who did? Yes. Who? Waskow.

What if the jury seemed unbelieving? After all, Marc's saying "Not me, him," could seem self-serving. The obvious answer was, I should testify, truthfully. Would I? Of course!

But one of the lawyers, looking me over, was unhappy. In those days I had a beard half-way down to my navel. I was the exact image of the crazed radical in the minds of the respectable Boston businessfolk whom the prosecutors would make sure got on the jury. I would infect their minds! No Waskow witness, unless absolutely necessary to save Marc.

Solution: I had to be in Boston for the whole trial but never in the courtroom. (Prospective witnesses weren't supposed to be there anyway, lest they be corrupted by hearing somebody else's testimony.) So I spent the time in the court library reading James Madison's notes on the convention that created the Constitution. It seemed just as pointed as Marc's insisting we visit Old South Church in Boston, where the Tea Party was planned and executed.

The 1767 Constitutional Convention violated, actually ignored, the provisions of the Articles of Confederation on how to amend itself, America's first constitution. The country needed something better; the Spirit called. They acted. The British monarchy enacted a tax on tea without the consent of the American governed. The Spirit spoke. The church and the people acted.

I was there in the court library, learning Madison, till June 5, when Marc was scheduled to be the next witness for the defense of himself and all the others. He woke up that morning to a phone call from Philip Stern, chair of the board of the Institute for Policy Studies and a member of the elected delegation from DC to the Democratic National Convention: Bobby Kennedy, only minutes after winning the Presidential primary in California, had been shot and killed.

Absorbing the news, Marc told me he would focus his testimony to the jury that morning on the plague of violence in America, with the murder of Bobby Kennedy as a terrible example of what he was trying to prevent.

The prosecutor pushed Marc on the charge in the indictment

that Marc had banged on a Fabrikoid briefcase in the Department of Justice, saying that the draft cards in the brief case were evidence of the crime of refusing to carry a draft card. Marc testified that he'd never touched the briefcase, banged on it, or said those words. (All correct; I did most of that, although I'd said the draft cards were evidence of what the U.S. government, not we, said was a crime.) Through all this, I was desperately wanting to get back to Washington to join my fellow-members of the Democratic delegation now mourning our Presidential candidate, Bobby Kennedy.

After making sure the lawyers thought Marc's testimony was powerful and mine would not be needed to back it up, I flew home. On the way, I started trying to figure out, who should now be the District of Columbia's candidate for president?

The chair of our delegation was a remarkable young Black minister. A younger edition of Martin Luther King, Jr. If we nominated him, he would be the first Black person ever placed in nomination for president at a major-party convention! Skilled in the best of political arts, as a well-regarded minister of a well-respected progressive church. A fine orator. A decent, honorable human being, as I would discover for myself at the coming convention. Committed to nonviolence. Opposed to the war. Actively engaged in dismantling racism. When I got back home and shared the idea, the delegates were excited. But some of the white antiwar liberals in our delegation practically begged us to meet with Senator Eugene McCarthy, the one remaining antiwar candidate. So we did.

One of our delegation opened by saying to McCarthy: "Senator, I am a welfare mother and I live in Barry Farms [then a Black very low-income project in the Anacostia neighborhood of SW DC, which was then the worst-off part of the District]. I'd like to invite you to come visit us and get to understand us." McCarthy responded: "I've been to the ghetto in Pittsburgh, and I know that every ghetto is like all the others. I understand already. No need to visit." The Spirit fell in shock and horror. The temperature in the room dropped thirty degrees. There was no chance we would support him.

I've wondered for years what made the Gene McCarthy of that moment so humanly disgusting and so politically stupid. I have a theory. He was well-known to have contempt for Jack Kennedy and probably for his brother. He once said, "They say Jack Kennedy is Catholic, smart, and liberal. Well, I'm twice as Catholic, twice as liberal, and twice as smart." Perhaps he was so angry at having to ask a Kennedy delegation to endorse him that he could not restrain himself. We are all scarred with some pustule of the anti-Spirit.

As we moved toward the Democratic Convention in August, various groups began to plan for demonstration there demanding an end to the war against Vietnam. The expectation was that in normal fashion, permits would be granted for anti-war rallies at several spots in Chicago and then near the Convention itself in the old stockyards neighborhood in South Chicago. (The stink of cattle blood could still be smelled in the streets there—perhaps a warning of the future.) But Mayor Richard Daley, who was also to be chairman of the Convention, stubbornly refused to issue permits, except a limited one for demonstrators in Grant Park just across the street from the Conrad Hilton Hotel. Many delegations to the Convention were housed at that hotel. The Illinois National Guard and special "anti-riot" detachments of the Chicago police force were mobilized and stationed in the street between Grant Park and the hotel.

The Convention was scheduled to begin on Monday evening, August 26. The day before, several delegates, including me, were contacted by Tom Hayden, one of the founders of SDS (Students for a Democratic Society) and a leader of plans for legal rallies in Chicago. Hayden was worried that the police and National Guard might charge the crowd in Grant Park. So he wanted a line of delegates to stand between the police and the park—hoping our presence would deter police attack. We agreed. Early Monday morning, Hayden was arrested. Delegates showed up at Grant Park anyway.

The songs and signs from the crowd turned out to be visible from the hotel, and many delegates in the hotel flashed their room lights on and off as a signal of support. We stayed till it was time for us delegates to head for the Convention. Somebody—I think it was Hayden, bailed out and semi-disguised in the crowd—asked us to come again Tuesday, and we agreed.

That Monday evening, the Convention received a report from its credentials committee recommending a "compromise" in seating both of the delegations claiming seats from Georgia: one led by segregationist Gov. Lester Maddox and one led by African-American state legislator and civil-rights activist Julian Bond. The antiwar, anti-racism crowd begin to chant, "Julian Bond, Julian Bond, Julian Bond"— and wouldn't stop despite repeated gavel bangs from Convention chair Mayor Daley.

Then Daley threatened to use the sergeants-at-arms to stop the chanting and allow the Convention to vote—presumably for the Credentials Committee "compromise." I was feeling history's echo from the Atlantic City convention and the Mississippi Freedom Democratic Party. I saw some delegates pick up chairs, ready to fight the sergeants-at-arms if they attack.

Perhaps Mayor Daley saw them too and blanched at the image of prime time television showing the Democratic Party breaking up into fist fights. So suddenly, amidst the chanting, Daley claimed to discern a motion to adjourn, recognized it, and declared it passed.

On Tuesday I headed again for Grant Park and again stood on the thin line between armed police and National Guardsmen and the unarmed demonstrators. Again, the atmosphere was tense but the line held. A theory then spread among us that Mayor Daley was concerned that if the demonstrators were allowed to march through the city to the South Side, when they reached those Black neighborhoods many thousand Blacks would join the march. Black and white together, they would become unstoppable without bloodshed. We didn't know what was in the mayor's head, only that we were committed to nonviolence and sickened by continuation of a brutal war that President Johnson has already admitted should end.

So the thin line of delegates went back to the Convention. Tuesday night was going to be dedicated to passage of the party's platform. Antiwar delegates had prepared an antiwar plank, with speakers ready to explain why the war was illegal, immoral, and destructive to America as well as Vietnam. We wanted to create a national teach-in with millions of prime time viewers.

But the Humphrey-Daley machine was bitterly opposed, and a whispered conversation came up with a deal: The antiwar plank would be voted on in a special morning session. Way fewer spectators, but the argument would be heard. Indeed, the debate took place on Wednesday morning, and a vote. The antiwar plank was defeated.

Wednesday evening, inside the Convention, would be nominations for President followed by a Convention-wide vote naming the Democratic Party's candidate for President. Our band of delegates who stood the line at Grant Park would be at the Convention for this climactic moment. And this was the moment the antiwar demonstrators had decided to march. The moment Mayor Daley had decided to stop them, at any cost.

What came was "Bloody Wednesday." Chants from the marchers, bloody and beaten by police and the National Guard. Chants of "The whole world is watching!" Scared and scarred demonstrators running into the Hilton Hotel, up to the campaign headquarters of the antiwar candidate, Sen. Gene McCarthy. What happened was policemen chasing them, beating them up, following them into the McCarthy offices. And then the McCarthy staff calling their delegates on the Convention floor to let them know what was happening.

The New York and California delegations, both antiwar, were side by side on the Convention seating plan. They quickly decided to call an emergency caucus of all antiwar delegates. Word came to me at DC, to delegates from Oregon, Wisconsin, maybe others. I went to Rev. Phillips, our delegation chair and our nominee for President. "Channing," I said, "I'm really sorry, but I may have to miss your nomination. The police are beating the shit out of the nonviolent antiwar demonstrators at Grant Park, even chased them into the hotel. The McCarthy offices called here, and there has been a call for an emergency caucus of antiwar delegates. These are my people; I need to go.

I don't know how long it will take, whether I can get back in time for us to nominate you. I'm sorry!"

Channing looked at me. "They are my people too! I'll go with you!"

"You are about to be nominated for president! You need to be on the floor, in the midst of the delegation!" I didn't even bother saying he was about to be the first African-American nominated for president in a major-party convention. He knew that.

"I'm coming with you," he said. And did. The Spirit rising in the wisdom of one young sage who understood that his own importance was closely bound up with the freedom and justice owed others. For me, all these years later, Channing Phillips' memory is truly a blessing.

The caucus was brief. The New York and California leaders offered a plan: We'd go through the alphabetical call of the states to nominate candidates, California would yield to Wisconsin. Wisconsin would move to suspend the call of the states, adjourn the convention because of the foul attempts at suppression of free speech and assembly, and reconvene in Madison, Wisconsin. There the streets would be Constitutionally open and the Convention would be free to make its decision—free from threats and coercion.

If Chairman Daley ruled the motion out of order, we would chant "Julian Bond, Julian Bond" as we had Monday and Tuesday evenings and force the Convention to adjourn. We took a quick vote, passed the proposal unanimously, and quickly returned to the floor. Channing and I were both there.

Reality rolled away much as the caucus plan had imagined. Then the moment came when Boss Daley ruled the motion to adjourn to Madison out of order. I held my breath. The chanting should begin now. But nothing happened. Or rather, the conventional order happened, moving toward a vote to name Humphrey the presidential nominee. I rushed over to the New York delegation and spotted Paul O'Dwyer, candidate for U.S. Senator from New York and a leader of antiwar sentiment. I asked, "Who is beginning the chant to force an adjournment?"

He looked at me with contempt. "They will never allow that," he said. "Tonight, they are nominating a candidate for President. They will never allow us to disrupt their moment."

I stood there, stunned. Slowly the truth percolated in my body. O'Dwyer could not imagine doing what the Southern racists were already doing—setting up a new party, nominating George Wallace for President, sowing seeds for the future. O'Dwyer could have gone home and run for the Senate as a champion of peace and decency and a New York break-through, the real Democratic Party. But it would have to come through broken chairs and maybe bones, through fist fights on TV. So he couldn't, because he wouldn't.

A line I had read somewhere ran through my head. It was George Bernard Shaw: "Must Christ be crucified in every generation to save those who are without imagination?" I extrapolated: "Must Jews be pogromed in every generation because some of us lack imagination?" "Must Vietnam be burned in every generation because some of us lack imagination?"

I wandered back to the DC delegation and sat down, exhausted and disheartened. I promised myself not to come back to the Convention on Thursday to see somebody named as Humphrey's running mate. In November, Humphrey lost anyway. So did O'Dwyer.

On Thursday night, so did I. I lost myself, foreswore myself. First, I went to Grant Park. It was almost empty, except for the strong smell of tear gas, and maybe one human being: Reverend Dick Fernandez, the executive of Clergy and Laity Concerned about Vietnam. "What now?" I asked Dick. He grunted: "Tonight someone will get killed in Grant Park." But he was wrong, because nobody showed up. Then I too decided to go, to not be one more dead casualty in this hopeless struggle for a democratic America and peaceful world.

First, my colleagues at the Institute for Policy Studies were sure that hundreds of Convention delegates would come for a free dinner to the Stockyards Inn, just a block or so from the Convention. Surely they would be ready to start a new party. I knew differently. It didn't take tear gas, just a perfectly decent liberal O'Dwyer, to convince me.

But I stopped in at the Stockyards Inn anyway. Nobody was there but my glum IPS colleagues.

Flying home next day, I counted the identities I'd lost. Peace-loving Democrat? Wafted away in O'Dwyer's silence. Street activist? Lost in gusts of tear gas and Fernandez' prophetic despair. Activist-scholar fellow of IPS? Useless, lost in the smell of Stockyards Inn steak.

9
The Freedom Seder

That April 4th changed the world. We all heard that MLK had been shot. It wasn't immediately clear whether it was fatal. In our house, the two of us grown-ups were very upset, and our four-year-old son asked what was wrong.

We explained that Dr. King, a very decent and good man and a great leader, had been shot and was badly hurt. Our four-year-old said, "He should have had a gun and shot first!" That's when Irene burst into tears and said, "He wouldn't have done that! He didn't believe in killing people, even angry, dangerous people."

I was supposed that evening to meet a Black woman activist whose name I can't recall, in a storefront office on 18th Street about a block up from Wyoming. I think she was an activist for "Democrats for Peace and Progress," our slate seeking election as DC's delegates to the Democratic National Convention. Still not knowing whether King might live or die, I walked up the street to meet her. I don't remember talking. She had brought a radio. We waited. They announced King had died. She said, "I guess we might as well leave; there won't be any volunteers coming tonight." I nodded. We left. I went back home.

The next morning, I was scheduled to be an expert witness for a hearing at the Customs Bureau on whether the film *I Am Curious, Yellow* should be allowed to enter the U.S. or be barred as obscene. Why me? The film had major passages about Dr. King, and I'd written a book called *From Race Riot to Sit-in*. I was intending to testify the film was an important documentary about nonviolence, including Dr. King's work. The hearing was canceled.

Not quite "instead," I was invited to speak at a memorial service for Dr. King at the American University campus on the far edge of DC. I spoke about how the President had spoken last night after King's death, urging that the Black community honor him and his legacy by acting nonviolently in response to his murder. I said that if the President really meant it, he himself—commander of an aggressive, illegal, immoral, brutal war—would order an immediate unilateral cease-fire by all U.S.-led forces in Vietnam. (King had called for an end to the war on April 4, 1967, exactly a year before he was killed.) I asked whether anyone would join me in a true memorial in content and process, by walking to the White House to call for exactly that. Thirty people did. I said that I was moved to walk all the way to the White House and call out to the President to do just that, and to keep the U.S. Army out of Washington. So we started walking.

When we arrived at Dupont Circle, about half-way, I suggested we pause for a bit, get some water and a little rest before moving on. As we did, a bystander asked what we were doing. I explained, and he blinked at me. Amazed. "Don't you know what's going on?" "What do you mean?" He pointed at the sky above 14th Street. It was thick with smoke. "It's burning!"

I explained to my co-walkers. I asked whether we still wanted to walk to the White House. Almost all of us did. When we got to Lafayette Park, for about ten minutes we marched up and down, chanting "End the war, NOW!" Then somebody said, "Inside, they probably can't hear us from so far away. Let's cross the street and march beside the fence!" So we did. At first, the police just watched. Then they charged us, batons flying. We were under arrest. The charge: Disorderly conduct. We paid fifteen bucks apiece and left. Some of us were ready for emergency work.

I mentioned that some of us weeks before King's death had smelled and tasted trouble in the air. We expected it to boil over in

July or August. And we put together skeleton plans for a center for emergency support. Support what?

Johnson sent the Army to occupy the capital city. It took longer than planned because the troops were in Virginia, across the river, and no Army official had expected the bridges to be jammed by thousands of whites fleeing the city.

Johnson also ordered a curfew. In theory it applied to everyone. The police enforced it against Blacks but ignored whites who were violating it by being on the streets. So we mimeographed permits for members of the center for emergency support—to be on the streets to give humanitarian support. That meant food, medicine, doctors, lawyers. Never once did a police officer demand to see our "permits?" Being white was enough.

For the week after Dr. King's death and the White House demonstration that's what I was doing: providing emergency support, day and night. Then came the first night of Passover. After my bar mitzvah ceremony when I was thirteen years old, the only Jewish festival I'd observed was the Passover seder. The festival was about resisting and escaping slavery to Pharaoh. The other holy days held little meaning for me. But as I made my way home on that bitter day, as I came to my block on Wyoming Avenue in Adams-Morgan neighborhood, I met an Army Jeep with a machine gun "guarding" my block. My kishkes, my guts, began to cry out at me: *You are about to celebrate freedom from Pharaoh, and this is Pharaoh's Army on your street!* So when I got home, I was awake as I had never before been to some words of the traditional Haggadah:

> In every generation, every human being (not just every Jew; *kol adam*) must see himself, herself, theirself as if they themselves, not their ancestors only, go out from slavery to freedom.

I had read that line ever since I was old enough to read, but only in 1968, after meeting Pharaoh's Army on the streets, did I read its fullest meaning. I did not yet know that, buried deep as a seed to grow in my soul, it was the call to write *The Freedom Seder*.

* * *

My life was transformed by that week between the murder of Dr. King and the first night of Passover. The violent victory of racism over the most effective and beloved nonviolent leader in American history was followed by uprisings in Black communities across the country. They were followed by repressive police responses and even military occupations of some cities—including Washington DC, the capital of the United States, where I lived. One week after Dr. King was murdered, the coming of Passover woke me up.

The moment of "awokening" came when I walked home to prepare for my family's Passover seder, retelling the ancient story of the liberation of the ancient Israelites from slavery under Pharaoh. As I approached my home, I saw a Jeep with a machine gun pointed at the block I lived on. From deep in my gut arose the words: *This is Pharaoh's Army, and I am going home to do the seder. This is Pharaoh's Army...* That moment was the turning of my life.

To what did I awake? To an earthquake inside me, and an earthquake all around me. Within me, the earthquake shook me first into transforming my understanding of Passover. From a pleasant memorial in words and foods and melodies of an ancient Jewish freedom struggle, it became a beckoning, an incitement, to all peoples now to win their freedom from all Pharaohs—and I found myself writing a new version of the ancient Telling—a Freedom Seder, we called it.

Soon the earthquake shook me into transforming my whole life, from a barely casual relationship to being Jewish to a passionate encounter with Jewish thought and practice. I found myself, beyond my will, reframing my life around Jewish teachings, symbols, festivals, and practices—ultimately, to becoming a rabbi.

* * *

As the trees turned color that fall of 1968, I turned to a task I had never imagined doing: writing a new haggadah, a new telling of my own for a Passover seder the following spring. I felt a powerful need to do it. I knew what the haggadah was. I'd been soaked in English versions of it every year since I was six and could read, and then an illustrated haggadah I received as a bar mitzvah gift.

It was about the liberation of ancient Israelites from slavery to Pharaoh, and my family thought it had a strong but vague teaching to seek freedom and justice. So as an adult when I abandoned all the other Jewish festivals, I still kept the Passover reading and the eating—the pressed-down flat-bread *matzah*, the bread baked hurriedly as the flight to freedom began; the fiery bitter herb, that horseradish that took away your breath and reminded you of the bitterness of slavery; parsley for what? maybe spring; salt water for what? maybe tears. A few other peculiar edibles.

My new haggadah must include powerful teachings about the modern pharaohs: those who blunted the efforts of the Mississippi Freedom Democratic Party; those who plotted the murder of civil rights workers, Black and white and Jewish, and then Dr. King; those who ordered the Army into Washington when the Black community rose up; those who sent the Army to kill Vietnamese; those who flattened the antiwar and antiracist movements at the Democratic Convention in Chicago.

In my new telling, I kept its archaic English renderings of Exodus and Psalms. But I looked afresh at the traditional debate among the ancient rabbis: Were there ten plagues, or twenty, or fifty, or 200? To me the notion of a debate seemed brilliant, the essence of freedom for a tale of freedom, but its content seemed silly. What would be a debate that would move and challenge modern people?

I decided on a real and current issue: would violence or nonviolence be wiser to win freedom from racism? I intertwined passages from King and Thoreau; Ginsberg and Gandhi; the Warsaw Ghetto Uprising against Nazism and the Nat Turner rebellion against slavery; the Christian radical pacifist A.J. Muste calling Moses the organizer of "Brickmakers Union Number 1," and a pacifist Russian rabbi named Tamaret who said the Bible was saying that no Israelite, only God, lifted even a fist against Pharaoh. Across continents and centuries as they were, I wove them all into a new telling of the tale of freedom.

I found myself doing something weird—stopping after writing a paragraph to call a friend to read out: "What do you think?" (I had written several books by this time, and never had I felt the need to check with my friends in the midst of writing.) Half my friends said, "Waskow, that's amazing! What an idea! Keep going!" The other half said, "You can't do that! There *is* a haggadah. Nobody can just write a new one."

That split happened so often I decided I had better check. Was I obsessed, crazy, or was this a good idea? I asked around for the name of a rabbi who would at least be sympathetic to the political debate. His name: Harold White. He was active against the war and against racism. I called him, described what I'd been doing, said I wanted a frank opinion: Was this crazy, or useful? "A least it sounds interesting," he answered. "Send it to me." A week later, he called back. "Waskow, I love it. It's an activist midrash on the haggadah. It's so activist that I wonder whether you know the ancient rabbinic midrash that God refuses to split the Red Sea until one activist goes into the water, up to his nose, about to drown?"

"What's a midrash?" I said. Silence. A pause long enough for me to steel myself against a polite, *Oh. I see. Um, It's a great idea. But perhaps a rabbi, or someone more steeped in Judaism, could carry it off and convince others.* But instead, what came was "Oh!," and even over the phone I could feel the excitement rise. "Let me share the midrash with you! The rabbis would take the ancient text and read it in new ways. On this one, where the Torah says the people 'went into the sea on the dry land,' the rabbis ask, 'Which was it? How could it be both sea and dry land?' And they answer that one of them went in while it was still sea; only then did it become dry land."

"You see? The people had to act. The rabbis took the ancient text into their own hands because they wanted the people to take future history into their own hands. The text at first glance seems to leave all the action to God; but the rabbis reread this oddity of text to mean the people acted. That's midrash. Your haggadah is new midrash. For God's sake, keep going! And let me share some midrash with you!" So he lent me an anthology of midrash collected by Nahum Glatzer called *Hammer on the Rock*.

I fell in love. The title meant that midrash was the hammer on the rock of Torah, and the living sparks of truth rose when someone used that hammer to hit the rock. And Rabbi White was telling me how that someone could mean me and other people now, not only some rabbis a couple of thousand years ago.

A whole new language that my heart had not even known to search for all these years, a whole new language I never knew existed. A language of transformation-through-renewal, a language that drew on an ancient language to make it deeply new. A language of serious play that could, with a wink and a twirl, turn reality in a new direction and claim it was simply uncovering a meaning that was already there. A language of puns, serious and funny puns that took as cosmic teaching the clang of words and phrases with each other. And this, the rabbi taught me, was what my new haggadah was already: a midrash on the ancient text that turned it in a new direction.

What neither he nor I expected was that as I was reinterpreting the text, the text was reinterpreting me. Turning me in a new direction, making a new "I" that was a midrash on the old me. Now I would say I was scooped up by the Spirit rising, tossed high in the air, the Breath, the Wind. But in 1968, I had no such language for what was happening. So I went ahead with the transgressive, transformative haggadah that eventually was called *The Freedom Seder*.

***

Warren Hinckle and Robert Scheer, co-editors of a well-known radical magazine called *Ramparts* came to visit Marc Raskin at the Institute. They sought his help in fundraising to keep *Ramparts* afloat. He gave them suggestions of whom to contact, and they were about to leave, Marc told me, when one of them stopped: "Is there anyone here at the Institute who's writing something *Ramparts* could use?"

Raskin said, "Well, Waskow is writing this very odd thing, a radical version of the Passover seder that celebrates the Black liberation movement alongside the old story of Israelites and Pharaoh." "Wow," they said. "Perfect!" So early in 1969 it was published in *Ramparts* magazine, where tens of thousands greeted it with joy: a religion they could share! And then Mike Tabor, the boldly creative leader of a small group of young Washingtonians called "Jews for Urban Justice" (JUJ), came to see me. "I hear you've written a radical haggadah. Very nice, but what's a haggadah without an actual seder?" "You're right!" I said. "What do you have in mind?"

"A big public seder. Maybe in a Black church. Would you be willing to do that? You have any contacts? Maybe on Dr. King's first *yohrzeit* [death-anniversary], which is actually during *Pesach* this coming spring. I looked it up."

"My God! Brilliant! Yes, and yes, and yes. As for contacts, I'm good friends with Reverend Channing Phillips. Maybe you remember? We—the DC delegation to the Chicago Convention—nominated him for president. He's the minister of Lincoln Temple. And he's a real *mensch*. Deeply gentle, deeply radical."

So on April 4, 1969, the first anniversary of Dr. King's murder and the third night of Passover, we held a Freedom Seder in the basement of Lincoln Memorial Temple. Rev. Phillips, Rabbi Balfour Brickner, a priest in the mold of the Berrigan brothers whose name I can't recall, Topper Carew, Mike Tabor, and Sharon and Fran Schreiberg of JUJ, and I were at the head table, leading from a tiny pocket-sized booklet that was illustrated by a Black artist, Lloyd McNeill. About 800 people took part, ate matzah and the bitter herb. Marc and his six-year-old son Jamie Raskin, my five-year-old son David Waskow, were among them. Jews and Christians, Black and white. It was broadcast live and whole by WBAI, the progressive Pacifica radio station in

New York City. An hour-long weave of televised excerpts was broadcast to all of Canada by the Canadian Broadcasting Corporation the following Sunday.

Over the years since, the experience of the Freedom Seder has stirred me to keep exploring new ways of understanding the Spirit. There is something about a gathering invisible, inaudible storm of new thought and action among more and more humans and other species that evokes a leap in public collective consciousness. I appreciate a metaphor from chemistry: If you have a super-saturated solution, you can drop one tiny crystal into it—and the whole solution will crystallize! I think that's what happened and is still happening with the Freedom Seder and its offspring, not just for Passover but also for liturgies and symbols and practices of all sorts that seemed frozen millennia go.

In our own world, very different from that of the Bible or the early rabbis, an urge toward a new model of religion arose and grew and grew till its intensity was at the saturation point. I dropped the crystal of the Freedom Seder into it, and seemingly frozen habits began to flow and change. If not me in the long year of 1968, someone else within a year or two. That is a non-hierarchical way to understand the Spirit rising.

What is more, we don't want the Spirit to rise and then get stuck. I realize that never again can the seder freeze. Now, again, we need a new Freedom seder. "In every generation" and even much sooner. What makes time and life into a spiral, instead of either a straight line or an endless circle, is setting aside time for reflection, rest, renewal. One curve that moves the spiral onward is that renewal time called Shabbat; each pause to bless Creation and say I-Thou before we behave as if the world is only an It; the Great Shabbat when, we are taught, we must let the Earth have its own restful year.

Now I understand midrash as a spiral, in which we go back again and again in order to go forward. We draw on ancient wisdom to create new wisdom. What went before, we turn and turn like a kaleidoscope. With every turn, new beauty, new patterns, new complexity. Facing new versions of the world. Birthing new versions of ourselves.

***

It took a phone call in the spring of 1970 to start me into the adventure of the Freedom Seder at Cornell University. The call came from a Cornell student. He explained that in honor of Father Dan Berrigan, there would be a long weekend at Cornell expressing opposition to the U.S. war against Vietnam.

Now, I have mentioned the name "Berrigan" twice already. Let me explain. Father Dan, a Jesuit priest, had been a deeply beloved chaplain at Cornell; he had become a vigorous nonviolent resister to the war; and he was now underground, resisting arrest by the FBI to face criminal charges for his resistance to the war.

The student who was calling explained that the weekend would take place during Passover. The organizers had heard of the Freedom Seder we held in 1969. They wanted to know whether I was interested in coming to Cornell for the Friday evening at the start of the weekend, to lead one on the campus. I said, "Of course I'll come!" And I made arrangements. When I landed at the Ithaca airport, two students were there to pick me up. They asked, "Would you mind if we went to see the Cayuga River falls before we take you to the campus?"

Every once in a while, as an amusement in my life, I had sung the various school spirit songs of various universities. Among them was, "Far above Cayuga's waters / With its waves of blue, stands our noble Alma Mater / Glorious to view / Lift the chorus, speed it onward / Loud her praises tell /Hail to thee our Alma Mater! Hail, all hail, Cornell!" So, was this a sacred initiation ritual for me as visitor, or for the week-end? Why not go?

We stood close to the falls, roaring as the waters fell. Then the students explained: "The campus is crawling with the FBI, wanting to arrest Father Dan in case he shows up. The only place we could talk without being overheard by their mics was here. The roaring of the falls masks all conversations." I blinked. (In silence: OK. This Freedom Seder might be even more exciting than last year's.)

Indeed. The students went on: "Suppose, just suppose, that Father Dan did indeed want to come out of hiding and take a public part in the seder. When do you think would be the right time?"

Woo-hoo! Me: "Early on, we say 'Let all who are hungry come and eat. Let all who are in need come to celebrate Freedom.' I think that's when."

They said, "We thought that was one possibility. The other one we thought of was when we invite the prophet Elijah in."

My mind raced: In Jewish tradition, Elijah comes just before the Messiah. In Christian tradition, John the Baptist was Elijah, proclaiming the advent of Jesus as Messiah. I admired Father Dan enormously. But Jewishly, do I want to name him as the messianic precursor? I don't think so. "No," I said. "I prefer the earlier time." They said OK. And off we went to the Cornell campus. The seder was held in the enormous Cornell Fieldhouse. There were a couple thousand people, sitting mostly in clusters on the floor. Each cluster had a paper plate with the crucial edible symbols: matzah, a bit of horseradish as the bitter herb, a sprig of parsley, and so on.

I thought to myself, this might be the biggest Passover seder since the Roman Empire's destruction of the Temple! I wonder how many of these folks have any idea what a Freedom Seder is. Maybe they think it's the name of a new rock band.

The designated leaders, including me, were seated on a stage, a few steps higher than the thousands sitting on the floor. Off we went, into the recitation. When we reached the passage I'd designated, a man who had been sitting on the floor, covered in a bulky overcoat that overshadowed even his face, arose, walked to the stage, climbed the steps, and took off the overcoat. It was Father Dan. The fieldhouse went berserk with cheers and clapping. Campus radio was broadcasting the seder live to dorms around the campus. Suddenly hundreds more students who had been listening on the radio came rushing into the fieldhouse. Many students came to the edge of the stage, sitting back to belly to make sure that no FBI agent could climb the steps to arrest Father Dan. They didn't try.

Father Dan joined in the recitation. About fifteen minutes later, a procession of eight-foot-tall puppets, each with a puppet-player inside the tall costume, came marching through the fieldhouse. They were the Bread and Puppet Theater, an iconic group that used the arts of puppetry and pantomime to oppose the U.S. war against Vietnam. They came up on the stage and mimed the Last Supper, which in Christian tradition was a Passover seder led by Jesus with his closest comrades. They finished and departed.

One of the organizers murmured to me, "I guess the Last Supper is the climax and conclusion of the seder." Under my breath, I thought, *In Christian theology, probably so. In Jewish theology, certainly not.* It's true that this is an interfaith seder, but interfaith doesn't mean the Jewish origins get swallowed up in another tradition.

Aloud I said, "There is still some of the Freedom Seder that we need to recite." And we did.

When next I glanced around the stage, Father Dan was gone. I had no idea when or how he had vanished, once more underground. It took me weeks to learn that as the Bread and Puppet Theater left the stage, one of the puppeteers had ducked out of his puppet and Father Dan ducked in. For one night, the Freedom Seder had actually liberated one human being. Weeks afterward, the FBI found where Dan was and arrested him.

We finished the seder—and the first evening of the weekend that the students had named "America is hard to find," after a book of Father Dan's. The weekend went on, and I stayed around. There was lots of rock music, and thick clouds of marijuana smoke.

I found myself getting unaccountably annoyed, even angry, and asked myself why. Finally, it came to me: every seder needs a bitter herb. Dan's presence and its reminder of the raging war had been our bitter herb. But now the bitterness had vanished into pure celebration.

Instead of the traditional Passover wine alongside the bitter herb, we had ecstatic song and marijuana.

I remembered Abby Hoffman saying that for the United States to outlaw marijuana was the same as the Soviet Union's outlawing matzah. For the Woodstock Nation, dope was a sacrament. A sacrament of what? Of the mantra "Be Here Now." And what did matzah teach? Three thousand years of history and struggle, in every generation against new pharaohs and for new freedoms. I thought, saddened, that "Be Here Now" was perhaps a truth for Shabbat. But I didn't think that mantra, on its own, could stick it out for centuries against the bitterness of war and slavery and pharaohs. Even with all its internal contradictions, its backslidings, the Jewish People would outlast the Woodstock Nation.

* * *

In 2019, The Shalom Center honored the long history of the Freedom Seder by holding a fiftieth anniversary celebration. We decided to magnify our commitment to inclusiveness, which was the whole point of the Freedom Seder in the first place, by holding it in Masjidullah, a mosque with an almost entirely African-American membership.

As a framework, we used Dr. King's definition of deadly triplets haunting American society. He named them as racism, militarism, and materialism. In the years after King was killed, sexism became more virulent in hostility to women, gay people, and queer people of all sorts. So we added sexism to the framework. We had Philadelphians who were intimately oppressed by one or another of these four quadruplets speak in detail about what it meant to their lives. And then we had Reverend William Barber, co-chair of the Poor Peoples Campaign, speak the climactic vision.

Donald Trump was president, and Reverend Barber took as his biblical text a passage where the prophet Jeremiah calls on the people to appear *en masse* at the palace of a corrupt Israelite king. As his oratory rang deeper and higher, he found himself not just recalling Jeremiah, but urging us to join with him at the corrupt White

House. And indeed, a few weeks later, thousands of people did join in Lafayette Park across the street from the White House to rebuke our corrupt and brutal "king."

We had arranged to have the entire seder filmed, hoping to create a documentary of a half-century. Pieces of it happened, but not the whole thing. We did transcribe Reverend Barber's speech in order to publish it in a book called *Liberating Your Passover Seder*. Phyllis and I edited the book, and Phyllis did the transcription of the speech.

She came to me with a puzzle. There were about forty seconds when Barber seemed to be speaking in what sounded like an intelligible language. It wasn't English, it wasn't Spanish, and it wasn't any other language she had heard. So I called him to ask him what those forty seconds might be. After a long pause, he said, "I grew up in a family that was Pentecostal Christian. Speaking in tongues was a sacred practice in the family. It was described as an echo of what happened when some followers of Jesus met him long after the crucifixion. All the followers began speaking in every human language whether they had known it before or not. In Christian tradition, that became the foundation of a trans-national Christian church."

"When I grew up and went away to a formal seminary to become ordained as a Christian minister, they told me that speaking in tongues was superstition. So I tried to stop. But every once in a while, there came over me the speaking, and it just flowed from me. That's what happened for those forty seconds in your Freedom seder.... There's one other thing I need to tell you. The Freedom seder was the first time in my life when the speaking in tongues came at anything other than a Christian prayer service."

Even months later, I could hear the Spirit humming a sacred song. Even now I can remember how it felt to have the Spirit celebrate a Christian prayer form that came unbidden into a Jewish and multi-religious sacred practice. Far from condemning the speaking as superstitious, I was honored that it happened on our watch.

10

Fabrangen

By 1970, several members of Jews for Urban Justice started to ask why we were not celebrating Shabbat. Rob Agus said to the more or less secular group of Jewish activists, "Shabbat is a revolutionary day. No money, loving community, thinking about the Torah of ethics, joining in celebration of the Unity of all. What could be more revolutionary than that? So why don't we try exploring what it would be like to take Shabbat seriously and celebrate it. We don't need an official rabbi. We can share with each other what knowledge we have and learn more as we go."

Rob was the son of a nationally known Conservative rabbi, Jacob Agus, with a long string of rabbis in his genealogy. I would say he was trying to invent the way that would outdo that whole list of rabbis without becoming one himself. He persuaded enough of us that it would be a great idea for a social action group to invent a new kind of prayer collective, the opposite of a synagogue inventing a social action committee.

So we went to Washington, DC's equivalent of a federation to ask for a grant to pay for rent and a couple of low-income staff for a Jewish collective near Dupont Circle, the center of cultural and political radicalism in the city. They said yes, hoping to save young Jews from all kinds of experimentation and bring them into Jewish community and practice, even though they knew it might be unconventional.

Then Rob knew he needed a name for this new enterprise. He

knew there was, especially in Hasidic circles, a Yiddish word that meant "bringing together." So he called his mother to ask how to spell the name of this new/old, old/new Jewish gathering. He knew, a little hazily, it was something like "Farbrangen." He thought his mother spelled it out to him as "Fabrangen." At least he didn't hear a first r, though in Yiddish that would have made more sense.

So he came back to us with this new name, Fabrangen. Afterward, when someone questioned the missing r, he said there were two reasons it wasn't there. First, pretty humdrum, was that he misheard his mother over the telephone. Second, the old Farbrangen meant a bringing together around a rebbe who would teach—but we didn't have a rabbi and didn't really want to have one person being a teacher. So the r we dropped was for the rabbi we didn't want.

That explanation turned a mistake into a meaningful assertion, and the Fabrangen opened in February 1971. It had three staff: Rob Agus; a singer and song writer, David Shneyer, now a cantor and a rabbi; and a young lawyer to act as anti-draft advisor for young students who didn't want to be drafted into killing and dying for the U.S. war against Vietnam. Not a conventional Jewish staff, even for the new *havurot* that had appeared in two or three cities around the country.

* * *

My fame or infamy about the Freedom Seder kept bubbling or doing what the pot does when it is too hot for several years. One of them was when one of the leaders of the New York havurah decided to try to bring together people from the two havurot in New York and Boston and me from Washington—I think because I was the only Fabrangener they knew about.

I said, "That won't work with us, with my comrades in Fabrangen! People don't view me as THE guy from Fabrangen. So if you are going to want people from the Washington havurah that is Fabrangen, you need to ask in some way the whole community. I know you can't bring the whole community to this event at the Rutgers University

Hillel, but somehow you need to ask the whole community." So he invited the whole Fabrangen, but said there was only room for at most five people. That left it to us as to which five. We named Max and Esther Ticktin, Rob Agus, Chava Weissler, who was a graduate of the Ramah Conservative movement summer camps, and me. We gathered at Weiss' farm in New Jersey. The farm kept kosher and it was a good place for serious Jewish groups to meet. And so we met people from the early havurot, the east coast veterans of the Havurah movement, and we worked out a very simple, useful and communitarian anarchist way of planning our meetings.

We decided we wanted to keep meeting and exchanging ideas. We decided we would meet on three long weekends every year. Usually, they wouldn't be Jewish festivals because the long weekends that were marked by U.S. holidays rarely fell on the Jewish festivals.

One of the benefits of the meetings was that I got to meet Arthur Green, the inspiring and organizing founder of Havurat Shalom near Boston. And in between our three pilgrimage festivals, in a new framework that borrowed from but was not the same as Jewish festival structures, I got to go to Boston to meet with Art and his wife Kathy. We sat on their front porch; I guess Art was probably still a graduate student at Brandeis University.

Just as we were shmoozing about our futures, I said, mournfully, that I realized I would never be able to read and fully make real biblical Hebrew the way Art and Kathy could read many levels and generations of Hebrew and Aramaic. I said that made me sad, because I realized there were many ways in which knowing Hebrew made a real difference. Especially in regard to writing a midrash where the playfulness of Hebrew, by just changing a vowel, can both affirm and transmute the meaning of the word. And I felt drawn, ever since Rabbi Harold White said my first draft of the Freedom Seder was an activist midrash, to the midrashic method to permit changes in interpretation.

Kathy interrupted me: "You're right. You'll probably never get to the Hebrew level where Art and I are. But let me ask you, how would you feel about spending maybe just two hours a week with Esther Ticktin learning biblical Hebrew?" I woke up from my glumness, "That would be wonderful!" So I went back home and called Esther and she agreed. A little while later, she got too busy and then Max agreed. I studied with Esther from a little book about biblical Hebrew and then for a year or so with Max from the same book that got more complicated as it went on. That conversation was a *m'chaye*—literally, a life giver. The learning opened up for me a life of joyful learning that midrash could transform the Torah. A definite rising of the Spirit.

* * *

In 1972, Rabbi Max Ticktin and Dr. (PhD) Esther Ticktin came to Washington for Max's new job as associate national director of Hillel—and joined Fabrangen. From then till their deaths, still Fabrangeners, deep in the twenty-first-century, I learned from them at many levels.

To begin with, it was an astonishment that they joined Fabrangen in the first place. Most Jewish leaders with a fancy new job in Washington joined a large and well-established synagogue. For the Ticktins to join a havurah that was less than two years old ,and then to behave like members—not "the rabbi" or "the *rebbitzen*" (wife of the rabbi)—teaching when appropriate and learning when appropriate, was exciting.

Then I discovered that Max, as a local Hillel director at the University of Chicago, had joined The Janes, an underground organization that gave help to women who needed abortions—when, before Roe, they were still illegal everywhere in the U.S. Indeed, for years he could not enter the state of Michigan because there was a warrant out for his arrest, on those grounds. That affected not only my understanding of the Jewish view of abortion but my understanding of what it meant to be a rabbi.

Then came deep learning from Max about the meaning of ritual. On Shabbat in most synagogues, one or a few congregants carry the

Torah scroll around the room just before the weekly portion is read. They make sure to come close to all the congregants, and many of them reach out to touch the scroll with their prayer shawls, and then kiss the shawl. I noticed that Max not only did this with his *tallit/* shawl; he also touched the tallit to the shoulder of the person who was carrying the Torah, and kissed the tallit. Puzzled, I asked him why. He answered, "For me, anyone who takes the trouble to carry a Torah *is* a Torah, and deserves to be honored like the Torah." In his memory, and in awareness of what he taught, I touch the carrier as he touched, kiss the shawl as he kissed. In Max the Spirit rose, and I try to rise with it.

※ ※ ※

After Max and Esther Ticktin had settled themselves into Fabrangen and into his new job at the national office of Hillel, Max offered to lead a discussion group about the Talmud. Every Shabbat we had read the traditional weekly portion in English, with comments and questions all along the way, whenever they occurred to people. Reading Torah this way sometimes took three hours. The discussion always centered on what this text meant to us and in our own lives, not to the great medieval scholars like Rashi or Rambam. For instance, what did we learn about our own relationships with our siblings from the repeated stories of conflict between an elder and a younger brother?

We would have a community-wide meeting once a month to consider our experience and our direction. One day in that monthly meeting, Esther Ticktin and Chava Weissler, two of our more Jewishly knowledgeable members, said that they wanted more time for prayer and even for lunch. They carried the day at least for more lunch; but there was also some muttering about the loss of time for learning with the Torah text. So Max offered to lead an open luncheon for weekly conversation with the Talmud.

We met in his apartment. We read Talmud together, commenting as we went just the way we commented on the weekly Torah portions. We thought about it the same way—reinterpreting its meaning in the light of our own lives.

One night Rob Agus said it felt to him like Torah was what God taught in the daytime and Talmud was like God's dream at night. Sometimes it would stay stuck on a single point for paragraphs and paragraphs. Sometimes it would wander into mystical fantasies. You could never tell where the dream would take you. Max said we were studying Talmud in a way that no other Jews had ever studied it. Making our midrash for our own lives as if it were Torah. We were continuing the Talmud, not just interpreting it.

In that group were three people who were on the steering committee of Breira, the first American Jewish group to urge publicly that the Palestinian territories Israel had conquered in the 1967 war, be freed to create a new Palestine at peace with Israel. That startled some people, annoyed some people. How could Jews who were studying this ancient "obsessive" dream-like document be the same Jews who were avowing such an unconventional, even radical, politics? They couldn't understand how what they saw as two different and contradictory worlds could mesh together. They did not know this was a sign of the Spirit rising.

I felt this puzzle splash in my face like ice cold water in my other life—at the Institute for Policy Studies. One day, Marc Raskin told me about a meeting that he thought would be good for me and for the Institute if I attended. I said I couldn't, because my Talmud group was meeting then. He looked at me aghast. "Talmud?" he said. "It's not an obscure study, but alive!" I said, hastening to reassure him.

***

In 1973, Father Dan Berrigan gave a public speech about Israel, a speech that became the cause, the explosion point, for one of the most trying emotional moments of my life.

Shortly after the speech, Fabrangen had what I expected would be a fairly humdrum meeting. But Dan Berrigan had sparked an explosive attack. He'd berated the State of Israel for its continuing occupation of territories it conquered in 1967, for approving and assisting settlement of Israeli super-nationalists in the territories, for its internal discrimination against Israelis of Palestinian heritage, and even for having not sponsored or encouraged any new creative social institutions that worked for the public good.

As that "humdrum" meeting of Fabrangen began, Rabbi Max Ticktin bitterly attacked me as if I had written Berrigan's speech, or at minimum, had done nothing to prevent it. There were three things, as I recall, that were the most explosive points in my friend Max's attack:

1. Berrigan's sentence saying that the State of Israel was responsible for "not only a dismal fate for foreign and indigenous victims, but the failure to create new forms of political and social life for her own citizens." That ignored the kibbutz and moshav, and I think was demonstrably false. It was only a secondary thread in the fabric of Berrigan's attack, but its existence invited a lover of the kibbutz to attack the entire speech as built upon bad faith.
2. That Berrigan used the number six million victims of Israeli oppression, which my friend and attacker said was a deliberate echo of the six million Jews killed by the Nazis. Maybe it was, and if so bound to stir not reevaluation but the kind of rage that was aimed at me that night.
3. Berrigan's quoting Eqbal Ahmed. I think that became part of the attack on me on the basis that Ahmed was loosely connected to the Institute for Policy Studies, of which I was a founder and one of the central faculty. To Max, this must've

> felt like I'd known what was coming and had been able to prevent or change it. But that thought was definitely not true; I thought and think that Berrigan should've consulted me, but he didn't.

Today, more than fifty years later, I have a fuller respect and a more trenchant critique of the speech Berrigan gave in 1973. It was "prophetic" in the sense that it described a great part of what Israel has become today. But it was not completely that in 1973; Rabin did respond in 1993 to the Oslo proposals, and by the time he was murdered had even become more and more fully a proponent of taking those proposals to their political destination, a two-state solution.

Berrigan's speech didn't treat the State of Israel in the way in which most of us treated the U.S. That is, a state about as legitimate and illegitimate as most other states, and worth struggling with to repair. We were, in fact, for instance, able to throw Nixon out of power. We don't know—if Rabin had not been murdered, or if his successor had gone immediately to the people to elect a new government, what kind of reform might have come, and how the state might have taken a profoundly different direction.

Rabbi Max was a person internally and externally free enough to look at his beloved Israel, see it sliding to the right, and join with other American Jews to try to counter that slide. A few years later, he was one of the group of American Jews, including me, who met with a small delegation of Palestinians from the leadership of the PLO. They'd come to Washington to meet with Jews in the hope of creating an initial atmosphere toward a workable peace. For the "Jewish establishment," the meeting itself was anathema, treason, heresy. Max and I had already reestablished our loving friendship. It lasted till his death in 2016. But the moment was searing.

In the moment of Max's attack, I was stunned into silence. Another Fabrangener said some words to re-incorporate me in the community. I was able to explain that I had had no fore-knowledge of Berrigan's speech. The Fabrangen's community meeting continued in its more or less humdrum way, though with the quiet thrum of an intense crash still reverberating.

Today, I believe that the deepest critique of Berrigan's speech was his misuse of the prophetic. The true prophet's word is almost always "if." There is almost always a choice, and the true prophet doesn't predict but calls for urgent change: "*If* this goes on, disaster; but you can change direction and save yourselves, and others, from moral degradation." Berrigan's speech did not sound like that to my friend-attacker, or to me. I don't think it helped us change Israel's direction at all.

* * *

It was not just Talmud that we got to study with Max Ticktin. One evening, with great excitement, he introduced us to a new translation of the Song of Songs. What excited him the most was that the translator—I'm sorry to say I can't remember who it was, but I think it came even before Marcia Falk did hers—was using Roman type for some of the Song and italics for other parts. That made it easier to distinguish whether a man or a woman was speaking. The Song suddenly felt like a conversation.

A love conversation. It could have been between two of us, out on a date together, describing each other's bodies lovingly. It could have been just the couple on a picnic together in the forest of Earth. Loving Earth's body just as much as we love each other's bodies.

We talked about how different this was from everything else in Torah or Talmud we had read together. Where the Talmud begins with a question of how early it is permissible to pray the morning prayers, the Song carries over and over the refrain, "Do not stir the lovers till they please." The spirituality of the one is tied closely to the clock and calendar; the spirituality of the other is loosely connected to the spirituality, the fluidity, of our own bodies.

"That was written by a woman," said one of us, herself a woman. "None of the rest of it was. Not even the book of Ruth, not even the Scroll of Esther, certainly not the Talmud with all its debates among male rabbis." I think it was the first time that any of us, even Max, had opened herself, himself, themself, to the Song. The Spirit rose and rose. Or maybe it is more truthful to say the Spirit deepened.

* * *

In January 1973, President Nixon had just seriously escalated the war against Vietnam by bombing North Vietnam's capital city, Hanoi, and chief port, Haiphong. Mr. Nixon was due to be re-inaugurated on January 20, a date required by the Constitution. The antiwar movement called for a massive counter-inaugural march on that day.

That day was also Shabbat. At Fabrangen, our members were unanimously and vigorously opposed to the war. So, what to do? We had a community meeting with a discussion that went on for more than an hour. Many different perspectives were set forth. First, Shabbat is a sacred time for reflection and inward rededication. Not a time for marching. Second, when we say Shabbat Shalom, are we not affirming the whole meaning of shalom? And does not that include taking part in this crucial action against the war? After a long conversation along these lines, someone said: "Tradition requires, not just permits, us to break the ordinary rules of *Shabbat* in order to save a life—*pekuach nefesh*. Isn't that what we would be doing by marching on January 20?"

At that point, Esther Ticktin spoke for the first time. She said, "Pekuach nefesh is about saving the life of someone who is close to dying, and who is present, in your face, where you can see death approaching, and where what you do can actually save that person's life. But we don't know whether taking part in this march will shorten the war even by one minute, can save even one life. I don't think we can say that marching carries out pekuach nefesh." She went on: "What I am feeling, and what I want to say, is this: 'Ribbono Shel

Olam (Master of the Universe), we know that if we take part in this march on Shabbat we will be violating Shabbat. We need to do it. Yes, we need to do it. Sorry!"

Our meeting erupted in cheers and applause. Esther, in her down-to-earth way, had spoken the real truth of the community, beneath the intellectual arguments. We marched.

11

Beyond God and Torah

The first religious service I ever led was at All Souls' Unitarian Church in Washington, DC, in 1967—before the Pesach after Dr. King's death in 1968 split my heart, soul, and life wide open—before I even imagined a serious Jewish life-path for myself, let alone the rabbinate.

The church had no minister that year and invited fifty-two people to lead one Sunday service each for that year. I was one of them. I was told I could change anything but the weekly collection for the building fund.

Though I had very little Jewish knowledge, I guess I had a Yiddishe *neshama* (soul), and two Jewish ways of thinking arose for me: whatever in the service couldn't be changed was the real service, and a service should arise from the tradition. So, what was Unitarian tradition, and what did it have to do with the collection of money?

I thought of Henry David Thoreau, who went to jail for refusing to pay taxes to support the U.S. war against Mexico. At this moment in 1967, my close friend Marc Raskin, along with Rev. William Sloane Coffin, Dr. Benjamin Spock, and a couple of other people—had been indicted for encouraging young men to resist the war in Vietnam by resisting the draft. I had been deeply involved in that work as well. So towards the end of the service, I invited the usual collection. And I said my sermon would be very brief because the congregation would have to write most of it. I quoted Thoreau on civil disobedience. I mentioned the draft-resistance indictments. And I asked the congregation to devote the collection to the legal-defense fund for the indictees. I said they would have to finish the sermon by deciding what to do. Then I left the pulpit and sat down in a pew.

There was a chaotic buzz, and the president of the congregation came forward and convened a formal meeting of the congregation to decide what to do. Some people urged giving the collection, as I had urged, in the name of Unitarian values. Some said it wasn't fair, people had given their money for the building fund. Finally, one member stood up and said—"It would not be fair to retroactively take the money that people gave with one purpose in mind, for another instead. But, how about taking up a new collection to give to the legal defense fund?" That's what they did. And I was told that three times the amount of money came in.

※ ※ ※

Reb Zalman is famous in my circles for having dared to experiment with LSD as a stimulus to spiritual experience. I had not. But I had the coincidence (or providence) that my first wife got to take part in a very distanced, scientific way, in research on LSD at the National Institute for Mental Health when that was still legal.

She taught me that "set" and "setting" were crucial to the experience. What people were told ahead of time and what atmosphere they actually experienced after ingesting LSD made a huge difference to whether their experience was delicious or disabling. So I decided to undertake the adventure with caution. I told Zalman I would like to take LSD with him as a guide. We arranged a day when his home would be otherwise empty. He prepared music, electronic art, and what he said was a reasonable dose. I took it.

Soon, I was standing at the foot of Sinai and as I looked toward the holy mountain, I saw an enormous multidimensional mirror. More than enormous: infinite. And in it, I saw myself and the whole Jewish people: thousands who have just trekked out of slavery; ancient Sarah laughing with her husband Abraham; my grandfather Pop, his yellow mustache shaking as he tells a bawdy story; some whose clothing I have never seen in history books. And I saw Egypt, Mother Egypt. And Babylon. And Rome. And India, and the Americas, and snowy plains of ice, and rolling oceans. The intricate web of human settlements, languages, cultures, dances; a hundred thousand foods, herbs, drinks of nourishment and ecstasy, the shimmering touch of hands and thighs and lips in delicate connection. And the glaring sun. Spinning planets. Whole whirling galaxies.

I saw my blood cells. One tiny red corpuscle. An atom of oxygen within it. Weightless positions, dancing in nothing.

All the while I was looking, I was also hearing. Echo: the infinite mirror, echoing one sound, one word: *Anokhi*, the elevated Hebrew word for "I." From all around me and from within myself, an overwhelming single word: Anokhi. It came like a drumbeat, again and again. This was clearly my I—my own self, but there was also no "my," no possessing, no being possessed. The I was the I that I am, and the I of an entire people. I spoke Anokhi as one voice of all the people. Again, again, Anokhi. I.

I saw the wilderness, I was the wilderness, the shimmering heat waves rising from its surface were my I, the spiral twirls of history, the woven tapestries of art and custom, the patterned laws of science: world upon world, infinity upon infinity, all I.

I saw myself, part of an unfathomable whole, not facing it but integrated in it. And for an instant I was infinitesimal, a tiny rhythmic breathing conscious cell in some vast breathing conscious ultrahuman. For an instant, I was infinite, containing in one enormous self all the worlds of fact and meaning. These instants were themselves a single instant, infinitely unfolding: they lasted for just a flashing moment, while stretching out for all eternity.

Then, Zalman heard my need, and responded calmly: "You will forget what you need to forget, you will remember what you need to remember."

I stood inside God's skull, behind the face; I looked out through God's eyes, my face in Face, I saw myself, ourself. Anokhi. There was no "Spirit." Everything was Spirit.

And reeling, stunned, I fell, rolled, stumbled away from the mirror in the Mountain, I closed all eyes and shrieked to see that I could still see Everything. With closed ears, I heard the voice still ringing in my bones; I backed away and tried to blot it out, forget. To not be I or we or anyone. And gradually I became a separate thou.

Gradually, I could begin to hear the I expand, contract, become "I YHWH your God Who brought you out..." I disentangled our selves, distinguished between the voice in their throats and the voice in my ears. Gradually they/I distinguished me/us/themselves from the ground beneath, distinguishing the pain in tightly clenched fists from pleasure in their open mouth, the breath within them from the wind around them, *Na'aseh*, "We will do...we/All There Is/will do," there is no Other. *Nishma*, "We will hear"...the Other speak to us.

I-Thou. As an artery channels streams of blood, there was only I; but then organic unity was gone. Connection was necessary. Gradually: Connections and commandments. "You shall keep Shabbat." "You shall not kill." From organic into what is organized; replaced harmonious wholeness with a plan, a patterning. Gradually distinguishing what they are doing from what they should be doing.

Ruefully I lingered, trying to remember the Anokhi and trying to forget it, relieved that I have been able to escape and joyful I will never be able to escape, already wishing to recreate the moment and frightened that the moment will recur without my wishing, still tingling, touching the impossible I have just done.

Laughing, tasting an apple, rolling on my tongue each drop of juice as if I had just returned to Eden.

※ ※ ※

In 1985, almost-Rabbi Jeff Roth was the executive director of a very loose and unconnected Jewish grouping that was scattered around

America and a few places in Europe, Latin America, and Israel. It was called *B'nai Or*—literally, "Sons of Light," though we took it as "Children of Light." These scattered groups had never met each other.

Reb Zalman Schachter-Shalomi was their only connection. He would go from city to town to college campus exciting people about the possibility of a whole new paradigm of Judaism.

Jeff Roth had the idea of bringing them all together for a weeklong retreat. Bringing us all together in one place and time meant that we would have to deal with issues where the scattered local communities disagreed. The place of gay and lesbian Jews in the broader Jewish community was a very hot issue in 1985.

The planning committee decided to hold a special session working to welcome gay Jews into the broader community. But the only people who went to that session were gay and lesbian Jews. After the workshop, an LGB caucus faced the planners: "We were the only people who showed up! Worthless! No use whatsoever. We didn't need to meet each other to know that we are fully human and don't need to be taught that. No point in talking to ourselves. Reach everyone. We demand a plenary session!"

We decided to set up a special session on differences in the community and make it the only session in the timeframe. So everybody had to go or sit by themselves, bored and alone.

The planners scrapped the original schedule and prepared a gathering with no competition to discuss "differences"—really minority sub-identities among us that might upset some of us. It would be led by gay and lesbian Jews, by people whose physical appearance might be unusual (like my bald beloved, Phyllis Berman), by people with physical or mental "disabilities." We urged everyone to attend. They did.

The caucus explored: how to make clear the gay presence is sacred, not heretical? "Let's do an *aliyah* (rising to honor oneself and Torah) to the Torah on Shabbat, honoring those who come out of the closet." Do we dare? Reb Zalman does. He offered to chant from the Torah for this aliyah. But when the weekly Torah portion included the prohibitions on gay sexuality, Reb Zalman chose instead to chant the passage, "Love your neighbor as yourself."

As the summer sun shone brightly, gays and lesbians, some unknown even to their friends, rose for the aliyah. Tears. Laughter. A transgender member of the community rose in self-revelation. The community exulted as a new face of God becomes visible.

Shechinah (feminine aspect of Godness) was reveling in her joyful unveiling, coming forth from her own closet. Celebrating us all for our midwifery of her and of each other, beckoning us to many more rebirthings. The aliyah was a success in numbers and spiritual focus. Some people made lavender triangles—a symbol of gayness reclaimed from humiliation under the Nazis, like the six-pointed star that the Nazis forced Jews to wear. (Its use preceded adoption of the rainbow as a symbol of gay pride.) Here it would be a freely chosen symbol for gay Jews and also for non-gay Jews who chose to announce they were allies and supporters.

We attracted joyful supporters as well as people who had never before told anyone they were gay. And we could hear Shechinah, the indwelling aspect of God, chant the blessings that precede the Torah reading. The Spirit rose and roused the whole community.

* * *

In 1987, Adina Abramowitz, one of the members of B'nai Or Philadelphia, led a Friday evening service for the community. She began by telling the story of her recent visit to Washington to join in shaping and celebrating the quilt that was a memorial for those who had died of AIDS.

She explained that from everywhere in America came squares of fabric, colorful and spirited. Thousands of gay people joined to take these squares and tie them together into one huge quilt. Adina used the word "grommets" over and over again to explain how the squares were tied to each other. This awoke me like a tiny candle flame in the midst of darkness. The only other time I'd seen or heard the word "grommets" was in the Torah's description of the making of the *Mishkan*, the holy shrine that the runaway slaves carried through the wilderness as a home for God. I began to think how like the ancient Mishkan was this modern Quilt. For years, I had read the thrice-told story of the building of the Mishkan, feeling bored with all the repeated detail. First, God sets up the first PowerPoint to show Moses pictures of what the Mishkan needs to look like, because words are not enough. Then Moses repeats it all to the people. And then the people bring the cloth, the fur, the dyes, the gold and silver, the olive oil, to shape the Mishkan.

Suddenly, I heard the Spirit rising up to whisper "grommets" over and over and over again. I began to see all of this artistic detail in a new, holy light. I saw the AIDS Memorial Quilt as the first public act of people's art from the previously hidden community of gay Americans. It re-membered the dead of AIDS, who had been ignored by official America even as they died in thousands. Coming together in Washington was exactly a statement of their visibility, and after grommeting the Quilt together, they carried it from place to place.

I never again found the Mishkan boring.

* * *

When I first wrote about Godwrestling, it seemed to be a dance of joy. A light with no alloy of darkness. Even the aspects of the Torah that seemed to me most dangerous—its subordination of women, its willingness to destroy whole peoples—seemed also possible to transcend. I still believe that. Yet all these years later, I have a deeper sense of how great the pain and how deep the danger that some aspects of Torah carry. I see now that, like Jacob, we might leave this wrestle with a wounded thigh. The same Hasidim who teach that the Torah is Divine Light also teach us that the only way to light is through darkness, that "There was evening, there was morning: one day." Creation begins in the dark of night; only then can it dawn. Streaks of dark remain forever.

I have twice experienced a moment of utter darkness in the weave of Torah's light.

The first came when Phyllis and I were leading a class on sexuality in the Torah at a summer institute of havurah people. We asked people to read as overnight homework the story of Dina in the first book of the Torah, *Bereshit*/Genesis.

Dina, the one daughter of Jacob who is named alongside his twelve sons, goes out to "visit the daughters of the land." She is raped by Sh'chem, one of the local Canaanite notables. He falls in love with her and asks to marry her. Jacob's sons insist that he and all his clansmen be circumcised first. Sh'chem and his followers agree. On the third day, when they are in the most pain from the operation, two of Jacob's sons fall upon them and kill them all. In the entire story, Dina says not a word.

Phyllis and I asked the class to be prepared the next day to speak in Dina's name. We were ready for a "drushodrama" ("bibliodrama" according to Peter Pitzele) in which Dina would speak first and then others might take on different parts. When we asked for first a volunteer to speak, a man's hand shot up. I blinked and said, "That's fine, but before you give your voice to Dina, I'd like to have two women have their say."

There was a silence. Then Judy Wasserman stood. She closed her eyes, then looked around the circle of our faces. "Raped. I have been raped three times. Once by Sh'chem. Once by my brothers, who did not ask me what I thought before they did this killing. And once by the Torah, which will not let me speak. Still by the Torah, which is still raping me." She began to cry and sat down.

There was a long, long silence. Finally, I said, "Is another woman ready to speak now?" There was a longer, longer silence. Then Phyllis said, "Is no one coming forward because you other women feel that Dina has truly spoken, that what we have already heard is really Dina's voice?"

All the women nodded. And Phyllis said, "Me too."

Raped by the Torah. Silenced by the Torah. What can anyone say? What can any man say?

Ever since, I have tried to keep that moment of darkness alight in my consciousness whenever I've wrestled with Torah. Even as a newcomer and an outsider, even as one looked down on by those who have spent a lifetime learning the elaborate process of Torah study, I could find some version of myself in the various stories. But I was never silenced; I was never raped.

What would have to happen for women to feel at home in these stories? Despite the darkness of that moment, I did see the light that sprang from it, just as the Hasidim said it would. For in the very same breath that our Dina was saying that the Torah rapes her, she was saying it by doing midrash on that very Torah. Perhaps the most radical imaginable midrash, for it utterly negated Torah at the very moment of affirming Torah. Affirmed it by negating it. Negated it by affirming it. The light could not be separated from the darkness. Smile away the dark discovery, and enlightenment would also vanish with it.

It was like running headlong into a Black Hole of utter emptiness, in the despairing hope that within the hole there is the birth of an entire universe, a billion galaxies.

Is there another Torah hidden within the one we have? Another Torah to be found only by plunging deep into the terrifying darkness of the one we read? The rabbis found "another Torah" in the white fire between the letters of the written Torah: the other Torah they called "Torah through the power of the mouth." (Most translators say "Oral Torah," but notice how they lose precisely the power of the mouth.) The rabbis said this Torah only seemed like new; it really came at Sinai, alongside the Torah of the pen.

And we clever modernists, we think they fooled themselves. We smile with admiration at how successfully they did it, but most of us cannot bring ourselves to believe that the "Oral Torah" came from Sinai. We think the rabbis made it up. Where does that leave us? Can we, historically sophisticated readers that we are, draw a new Torah from the silences within the old one, as they did? Or are we too smart to fool ourselves, as we think they fooled themselves? Are we too smart to be successful?

* * *

Seven weeks of walking from the narrows into the open space that is the land of no one, and then we enter the heart of the heart of the wilderness—Sinai itself, and the Torah.

"Wilderness" is *midbar*. It could be understood as *midaber*,—"wording, speaking," or *m'devar / m'dibbur*, "away from word, without a word, beyond words." Or both: a speaking beyond words.

Several years ago, Phyllis and I spent a few days in midbar Sinai, and with hundreds of pilgrims from many religions and from all around the world spent all night climbing the mountain that either is or isn't the mountain where we all assembled to get the Teaching that was beyond words. For as one teaching about the Teaching goes, no word at all was spoken—only an *aleph*, the first letter of the Ten Words that have come down to us.

The aleph, the silent sound made by an open throat. From just the truth that the universe wants to speak with us comes all the rest, for us to figure out: don't kill—don't take a useful part of the whole and carve it out from all the flow, rigidify it and bow down to it—

When we looked out at dawn and the many diverse pilgrims began to sing and sob in joy, Phyllis pointed to the nearby mountains. "See," she said, "the Tablets!"

The mountains themselves, in their geological formations, look like the conventional images of the Tablets that we see in our art and on our synagogues—and running across them are horizontal outcroppings, grooves, furrows, horizontal bands of rough out-jetting rock separated from each other by horizontal bands of smoothness. Layer on layer, the outcomes of convulsive wordless history. Outcroppings that can almost be read. Beyond words.

The Tablets of the earth itself and the Utterances of the earth itself. Torah.

* * *

One of the most important things we did in the long struggle to renew and maybe even transform Judaism was the investment by Rabbis Jeff Roth and Joanna Katz in creating a Jewish Renewal retreat center called *Elat Chayyim*. Its name could be translated, "Pistachio Tree of Life" and that's what we told people it meant. But it could also have been understood to mean, "Goddess of Life." That was the secret underground message.

Rabbi Roth as executive director of the retreat center, Reb Zalman as lead teacher, Rabbi Phyllis Berman as program director for twelve summers, and me as in-between Reb Zalman and all the other teachers were the planners and organizers of the retreat center, bringing rabbis, artists, musicians, all sorts of creative people to teach and to learn. On Shabbos, we used to sing a song that extolled the spiritual brilliance of *Yerushalayim* (transliterated Hebrew for "Jerusalem"), and after singing the first verse and its chorus, some of us would sing the rest of the song, with Elat Chayyim in the place of Yerushalayim.

It brought together a wonderful burst of Jewish creativity including the first generation since Sarah, Rebecca, Rachel, Leah, Zilpah, and Bilhah in which women had a full equal place in learning and teaching, and the shaping of a Judaism that was open to their wisdom. Indeed, a Judaism in which their teaching was foundational. Elat Chayyim taught hundreds of people that you could stretch Judaism in new directions without wrecking it or losing it.

I had as my mission leading the study of each week's Torah portion before Shabbat morning service. Sometimes I would start with a teaching of my own and invite responses from the community. Sometimes I would start with a connection between part of the portion and the lives of the people in this generation.

One day I was invited to a Reform Jewish summer camp near Elat Chayyim to share the work that The Shalom Center (see Chapter 13) was focusing on how to heal *adamah* (Earth) and *adam* (human earthlings) in what we call the climate crisis. Could they be woven back into a loving relationship of the kind that is described in much of the Hebrew Bible? I came back to Elat Chayyim feeling I'd failed to do that sharing well. The camp counselors were vaguely hostile. Some of the students seemed drawn to the idea, but many seemed not to get it. I went to sleep feeling disappointed and distraught.

I woke up the next morning with words for a sparkling vision of what the next seven generations of Jews could do along with others to save Earth from utter devastation. It felt like a *haftarah* (prophetic reading after the Shabbat Torah portion) I had been gently dreamed into. I went to Reb Zalman. "I think I've been given a new haftarah," I said. "Would it be ok if I shared it instead of the regular haftarah for this Shabbat?"

Said Zalman, "If you think you've got a new haftarah, let's hear it!" So I wrote down what I thought I received, and the very next Shabbat I spoke it, traditional blessings and all. Afterward, one of the community said he touched me for an instant and felt like an electric spark had flashed between us for a moment.

Zalman translated it into Hebrew. And I kept the words I received as a haftarah to be used on *Shabbat Noach*, when we read the rainbow covenant between the Breath of Life and all the living beings who breathe each other into life on planet Earth.

※ ※ ※

In 2003, Phyllis and I decided to take part at the Kirkridge Retreat Center in what was billed as a learning for religious opponents of the U.S. war against Iraq. The lead teacher was Sister Joan Chittister, Benedictine nun and a renowned feminist—an uphill climb in the Catholic Church.

When we got there, everybody else turned out to be Christians.

A new experience for us, and we waited openheartedly to learn what a feminist Catholic nun would teach.

What she taught was wonderful—and all of it was from what Christians call the "New Testament." We found ourselves bringing insights from the Hebrew Bible. Joan cheerfully gave us space and excited interest. At the end of the retreat, she told us that Benedictine nuns from all over America would soon be gathering for a week at the mother house in Erie, Pennsylvania. Would we come and teach Torah for the week? Of course we said yes.

What we taught, the nuns said, was rich and stimulating. What we learned was amazing. The Erie nuns had created an extraordinary array of spiritual activism. At its heart, Joan as mother superior taught fresh and unrehearsed three times a day as they gathered in prayer.

There was a ritual committee called "Fools on the Hill" that shaped new, quirky, and feminist liturgy. There was a committee whose work was to seek out orphans in the city of Erie, adopt them as children of the sisterhood, and raise them with love and tenderness. There was another committee that cared for older sisters from all over the country, also with love and tenderness. There was an on-campus office of Pax Christi America, a peace-activist organization rooted in Catholic social thought. The Benedictines contributed secretarial and other support.

At the end of our week, Phyllis in joy and laughter said that if she weren't already married, she would become a Benedictine sister. And the sisters gave us to take home a sign for our front porch: "Nuclear-Free Zone." It still hangs proudly to greet every visitor.

***

Reverend Hal Taussig, a radical Protestant minister, called me. He had in mind a new radical project, and he wanted two rabbis to take part: Nancy Fuchs Kreimer of the Reconstructionist Rabbinical College, and myself.

What was the project? To examine and vote to create from

ancient texts *A New New Testament!* Texts that had been ignored or deliberately excluded by those who decided on the Christian canon. About fifteen Christian preachers and scholars, plus two Jews, would vote to choose from a batch of texts that Rev. Taussig would present to us.

For a bit I wondered what it meant for two Jews to vote on a new Christian canonical collection, and then I figured the original writers certainly, and even the canonical decision-makers probably, had a number of Jews among them. Anyway, Hal had a publisher in hand for an English translation of whatever we voted for, under his provocative title. Why should I *kvetch*?

We met in a hotel room in New Orleans. One by one we read what Hal presented and took notes to prepare for a final vote. To me the process felt intellectually awesome, but not emotionally passionate. Then Hal lifted another text. It was from a collection that scholars called the Gnostic library at Nag Hammadi. He said its title was "The Thunder: Perfect Mind," but we could ignore that, for it had nothing to do with the content. He also said it had no Christian references or context. That intrigued me: *Why then is he proposing it?*

We read it aloud. To me, it felt amazing. There were more than fifty verses, almost all of them affirming a woman's life and practice. Each verse started with "I," but each verse contained a paradox. It affirmed two roles of a woman that were contradictory: "I was never married, and my wedding was a joyful celebration." "I" again and again asserting paradox or universality as expressed through difference, again and again and again.

The translator was among us. I turned to ask her, "What is the Coptic word that you have translated over and over as 'I'? She said, "*Anokhi.*" That was the word that began the Ten Utterances in the Hebrew Bible. Just once. In the Ten Utterances there is no paradox. It is simple and direct: "I [*Anokhi*] brought you out of slavery. Keep Shabbat. Don't steal. Don't murder. Don't envy."

But the world is full of paradox. I could feel Spirit ripping away the curtain that had hidden this text from us Torah-lovers, Torah-wrestlers. It fit an empty space that Dr. Judith Plaskow, a leading feminist Jewish scholar, had pointed out in her extraordinary book, *Standing Again at Sinai*. She noted that Torah seemed to posit a woman-space at Sinai, separate from the men. The Spirit whispered to me that women could know this hidden truth of paradox precisely because they were forbidden to be powerful.

Later, when I told Rabbi Jill Hammer, cofounder of the whole new lineage of *Kohanot*, Hebrew priestesses, of my discovery of "The Thunder," she said, "Oh! You mean the Goddess text!" I laughed. So clear to these new/old priestesses. So hard for me to discover.

I told the assembled Christians that this "I" (*Anokhi*) was from Sinai and its name came from the Thunder that Torah records from the encounter at Sinai. "You mean it's a midrash on Sinai?" said one of the Christians.

"No, it *is* Sinai. Part of Sinai," I answered.

"But there's no indication it's Christian. How can we put it in *A New New Testament* for Christians?"

"Look," I said. And I could feel the Spirit putting words in my mouth, urging me on: "Suppose you take it to the deputy librarian of Nag Hammadi, and he says exactly what you said, and turns it down. But you are stubborn, and you bring it to me. I'm chief librarian of Nag Hammadi, I read 'The Thunder' and I say I don't give a flying fuck at the moon whether this is not Jewish, or not Christian, or not pagan, or not some other label they will or won't stick on a library card 2,000 years from now, some made-up word like gnostic. It's clearly sacred. It's clearly divine. I want it in my library."

And the assembled religious experts voted unanimously that it belonged in *A New New Testament*.

***

For more than twenty years, I have learned to unlock ancient Torah with a postmodern key: the lives of about twenty-five companions who gather each Shabbat morning. We examine their/our own memories in the light of a Torah passage from the weekly portion and explore ancient Torah in the light of our own lives.

We do this in the atmosphere that "torah" comes from the language of archery in Hebrew. There it means "aiming the arrow"—not hitting the bull's eye, but in all good faith and effort, aiming. Though Hebrew has no capital letters, in translation, when "Torah" gets a capital "T" it means "aiming toward wisdom."

When our community reviews and refines our own memories, those too become "Torah." And for the whole process, we can feel Spirit present.

12
Reconstructionist Rabbinical College

There was one very small species of the creative Jewish variety that emerged in Washington: the Institute for Jewish Policy Planning and Research, led by Ira Silverman. He was a young Jewish entrepreneur with a reputation for saving Jewish institutions about to run out of money. He asked me to speak at a few of his seminars. But our connection would not end there.

When the founding president of the Reconstructionist Rabbinical College (RRC), Rabbi Ira Eisenstein, retired, the College, then very small, unfunded—started looking for a new president. The most obvious choices were not interested in saving a penniless rabbinical college. So the RRC board contacted my old friend, Ira Silverman, who was known for saving such Jewish places.

He said, "I have not been a Reconstructionist. I have to read Kaplan's work." That's Mordecai Kaplan, the Conservative rabbi whose teaching inspired the founding of Reconstructionist Judaism in the 1950s. They said, "That's fine." He said, "I will bring new people, like Arthur Waskow." I was still known best because of *The Freedom Seder* as a real troublemaker. They said "That's fine. Just save the College."

So he was chosen. In 1981, he was named the second president of the Reconstructionist Rabbinical College. As promised, he came to me and to others who would never have been invited by strict Reconstructionists. These included also Herschel Matt, a very creative Conservative rabbi, and the veteran outreacher for and then heretical exile from the Lubavitch community, Reb Zalman Schachter-Shalomi, leader of what was then called B'nai Or.

I had to decide whether to stay in Washington with no prospect of raising money for the creative Judaism I'd come to love, or for the political projects I'd helped nourish, and where I'd raised my children. Or move to Philadelphia, where I had just been offered a salary doing what I loved, where I knew very well a few people in a creative neighborhood called Mount Airy where there was a popcorn population of students of Reb Zalman, graduate students of professor Arthur Green at the University of Pennsylvania, Reconstructionist rabbinical students and faculty, and members of a multi-valued havurah nourished by the Germantown Jewish Centre. I chose Philadelphia. For me that meant the Spirit, so fallen in my departure from the Institute, could start to rise again among a bunch of maverick student rabbis.

*　*　*

The invitation to join the RRC faculty meant a major change in life. A change of home city from Washington to Philadelphia, a change from a mixture of secular activism and theory with Jewish thought and activism to an overwhelmingly Jewish orientation, even a change in the body of my close friends who now centered in Philly's West Mount Airy neighborhood.

I tumbled into a much more intense Jewish life than I had expected, beginning on Rosh Hashanah in September 1982. The Jewish year began with a retreat led by Reb Zalman at Fellowship Farm, a retreat center nearby. He called us "Yavneh II" after the gathering of early rabbis in the town of Yavneh during and after the Roman army's destruction of the Temple in Jerusalem. Their leader, Yokhanan ben Zakkai, wanted to establish that the gathering of rabbis at Yavneh was as sacred as gathering at the Temple in Jerusalem had been, and basic new rules of spiritual practices were necessary. He ruled that although previously it was forbidden to blow *shofar* (ram's horn) if Rosh Hashanah coincided with Shabbat—unless the shofar and its sacred sounders were in the Temple—that the same rule would apply in Yavneh. Likewise, if we were Yavneh II, the precedent should apply to us, and we should blow the shofar at that retreat on Shabbat Rosh Hashanah.

But Zalman would not. I asked him why. He answered, "I guess I just don't have enough *chutzpah*."

As we walked from the *davening* space to lunch, another participant in the retreat plucked my sleeve. "I don't get it," he said. "If you believe that we are reinventing Judaism like those rabbis in Yavneh 2,000 years ago, why don't you blow the shofar yourself? Sounds like you do have the chutzpah." I answered, "I've never been able to get a peep out of the shofar. I guess if the one who might won't and the one who would can't, the time has not yet come."

The next morning, as we rose for the second day of Rosh Hashanah, Reb Zalman took me aside. He said, "The staff of Fellowship Farm came to me this morning with a copy of the *Philadelphia Inquirer*. The whole front page and more inside are about a massacre of Palestinian refugees at Sabra and Chatila in Lebanon—a massacre carried out by Maronite Christian Lebanese, not by Israelis. But the Israeli army was sitting on the hill just above those refugee camps and their commander ordered them not to intervene. I think we need to deal with this this morning as part of Rosh Hashanah and I want you to be the one to lead us in dealing with it."

I took a minute to read part of the story and then I said to Zalman, "I am willing, but if I do it, I'm going to do it by making this whole article the prophetic haftarah for the day. After all, who's a prophet? One who sees the truth and then tells it. That's what this story is. If you want me to do it, that's what I'll do." He agreed.

When we moved back into the davening space, and got to the point in the service when we would hear the prophetic teaching, that is what I did, haftarah blessing and all. People in the assembly began to cry. But one of them said to Reb Zalman, "Yesterday you talked with us about reincarnation—that the dead will live again. So are these deaths really so terrible?" Zalman paused before he answered, "Maybe so, but first you have to *schrei,* [scream out] GEVALT!!"

So my time as an officially acknowledged teacher of Judaism to students who were becoming rabbis began with a tumult in the Jewish world. What was it "Jewish" to do? Obey whatever a general ordered, or act even on Rosh Hashanah, to save lives. For Zalman, it was clear: his chutzpah was limited when it came to blowing shofar, but saving lives knocked down all the walls of chutzpah that might stop him. Or us.

A few days later, the RRC faculty held its first formal meeting of the year. Meanwhile in Israel there had suddenly emerged a movement demanding that a special commission be convened to investigate the actions of the general and army battalions standing above the refugee camps watching the massacre. So at that first faculty meeting, I had the chutzpah to move a resolution at the faculty supporting the calls to the president of Israel to convene such a commission, and we'd send a telegram to the president with our opinion.

Ira Silverman, college president, intervened: "I don't think it's quite proper for the College to send such a letter, but I think it would be totally proper to send a letter signed by each individual member of faculty who wishes, saying that they are members of the RRC faculty." There were nods all around the table, so we did it. We sent the letter, signed I think by every member of the faculty, and the commission was called and its report interrupted, though it did not end, the military or political career of General Arik Sharon.

Meanwhile, one of my friends who lived in Philadelphia had heard that a professor in the religion department at Swarthmore College was due for a sabbatical year off, and the college had not yet found a qualified substitute. She suggested me and they asked a few questions. The first semester was scheduled to be a course about Martin Buber, the great Jewish philosopher of the twentieth century. Did I know enough about Buber to teach about him? Yes, I had read, so far as I could tell, every word of Buber's in English. Over and over, actually. Second question: Did I have a PhD? Yes. It was in U.S. History but all they cared about was that the label would be there, not disgracing the department of religion. So they hired me and I had the double joy of teaching bright and passionate students at RRC and Swarthmore, both.

But I didn't want the course to be "about Buber." That would turn him into an *"it."* He was the great proponent of a philosophy of I-Thou where the crucial question was the hyphen—the connection between one human being and another, or even one human being and a tree. So how did I make sure that this course was a conversation with Buber, not about him, even though he had been dead since 1965? I shaped it to read from Buber aloud, as if we were reading Talmud together in the traditional way; and we would stop whenever anyone in the class or I wanted to raise a question; and then we would talk with each other and with Buber.

One of Buber's books that we read this way was his book called simply, *Moses*. When someone asked Buber why he wrote what you might call a theological biography of Moses he said that he always wanted to have a deeper conversation with God, and figured Moses had the deepest. So maybe he could eavesdrop on that conversation and learn and do better in his own conversation with God.

We were reading the chapter of *Moses* called "The Words on the Tablets." The tablets, of course, were those of the Ten Utterances. But Buber skips the first two words: "Anokhi, I" and "YHWH." I had never really had a direct encounter with "YHWH" since my grandmother, teaching me Hebrew when I was eleven, told me to think and say *"Adonai*, LORD" when I read "YHWH." I protested that the letters were not there to make it sensible to make it Adonai. She said, "I know! Just do it!"

So sitting there in the class, trying to converse with Buber as Buber tried to learn how to converse with God, I said to myself, "What would happen if I really pronounced YHWH the way it would actually sound?" So I tried, and out came just a breath. My first thought was, a breath—that makes sense, that's the only sound that every human being in every language makes with every one of the sacred Names of God, of truth, of love. I felt as if I'd opened my mouth and the Spirit spoke directly in me, from me, into me, all around me. Just a breath! (In Hebrew, "breath" and "wind" and "spirit" are the same word—"*ruach*.") What would happen if we took seriously that God does indeed intertwine all the cultures? But we are intertwined not by lordship, kingship, and control, but by the breath that every human breathes in and out?

What came to me next was, it's not just human languages. Every animal, every plant breathes. The interchange between plants breathing in CO_2 and breathing out oxygen with animals breathing in oxygen and breathing out CO_2—that's what keeps life alive on Earth. This became a theology that grew and grew as I grew more and more with my students and peers and teachers at RRC and Swarthmore and everywhere.

But there was a third thought that came to me in a rush at that moment. I thought, it's right there in the siddur, the prayer book. "*Nishmat kol chai tivarech et shimcha*, [*Yahhhh*] *eloheinu*. The breath of all life praises your Name because your Name is in fact the breath of all life." So I'm convinced that's what "YHWH" meant in the Bible—"Breath of Life." But the ancient rabbis, overawed by the Roman emperor, dealt with their awe by telling everybody YHWH meant Adonai, LORD.

Then there came to me a midrashic tale. I imagine that one of the early rabbis had this insight about the breath of all life and he told it to his friends and they said, "That's amazing! You must put it somewhere where our communities will never forget it." So they put it in a special place in the prayers for Shabbat. And what do you know, once it was in the prayer book, everybody could just read it and forget it. That's the irony of trying to put the Spirit in a book. In such a book, you need to dig beneath each line, rediscover the feelings in the roiling gut and belly beneath each line, the whirl of confusion in the brain as a new idea takes form.

At the end of the course, the students thanked me and said the course was unlike anything else at Swarthmore. I met with the department chair to explore whether I could keep on teaching. He looked at me frostily, told me he had heard the course was unlike anything else at Swarthmore, thanked me, and said goodbye. Oh well. Sharing with the students more loving chutzpah than the administration could absorb had been worth it. I sighed and said goodbye.

I learned from those first few months in a new city, with a new profession, new friends, and a new life, that chutzpah was good as long as I was willing to see it as infused and tempered with love. Love of and for and from my new friends, with whom I shared a vision.

***

"Which is greater—study or action?" is a question in the Talmud. "Study, if it leads to action," responded Rabbi Akiba.

During the academic year of 1982-1983, I learned several non-academic truths. First, President Ronald Reagan and the Soviet leadership were renewing the nuclear arms race that had been mostly dormant since the missile crisis of 1963. Second, the U.S. Catholic bishops were inspired to issue a pastoral letter calling for a "nuclear freeze." That meant stopping the arms race where it was: no new nuclear weapons. Third, there were several Jewish funding sources— notably Sidney Shapiro at the Max and Anna Levinson Foundation, and Micha Taubman, an heir to an Oklahoma oil fortune, who were embarrassed by the absence of an outspoken Jewish voice about nuclear arms. And fourth, President Ira Silverman of RRC was deeply concerned by expanding nuclear arsenals and was head of the New Jersey Campaign for Nuclear Disarmament. Moreover, he hoped to create several centers as parts of RRC that would carry Reconstructionist ethical concerns into action.

I had written two books and edited a third about the varied and contradictory plans for nuclear "deterrence" and possible approaches to disarmament. So RRC submitted a proposal for a startup grant for "The Shalom Center" to the Levinson Foundation. Sidney Shapiro, its exec, called me. "Why should it be you instead of the Reform or

Conservative organizations?" I answered, "If you give it to the Reform folk, the Conservatives won't play; if you give it to the Conservatives, the Reform won't play. But if you give it to RRC, we are small enough and new enough that nobody is afraid of us." "Hmmm." said Sidney. "That makes sense."

The grant came, with one proviso: we were to work only on the nuclear question. We invited a decision-making board that included a few of Ira's pals from the American Jewish Committee, and Reform, Conservative, Modern Orthodox, and Reconstructionist notables. By 1983 we were off and running.

One new approach that I pursued: Jewish grounding for limiting or eliminating nuclear arsenals. I found and applied an ancient rabbinic midrash: Abraham, watching fire consume Sodom and Gomorrah for their sins, thought the whole world was going up in flames. "YHWH," he cried out, "After the great flood you promised never again to destroy the whole world!" Then he paused. "Wait! You promised only there would be no desolation by water. Surely you would not destroy it by a flood of fire!" And God was silent.

But in 1984, the Spirit spoke: The midrash had entered Black American tradition by way of song—"God gave Noah the rainbow sign. No more water, the fire next time." And then by James Baldwin's book, *The Fire Next Time*.

So The Shalom Center drew on the danger of a flood of fire as a nuclear holocaust. We never used the phrase "nuclear war." We explained that whereas an ordinary arms race might make it possible for the "winner" to win the race and then the war, piling up more and more and more nuclear fire would only increase a nuclear holocaust that would consume all Earth. On that basis we supported a nuclear freeze against the flood of fire, developed "Rainbow Sign" day—27 Iyyar, the end of the biblical flood—as a celebratory day in the Jewish calendar, and developed other Jewish practices as anti-nuke spin-offs from the story of the flood.

In the midst of all this, Ira Silverman left RRC to become director of the 92nd Street Y in New York City. His successor, Rabbi Arthur

Green, was not interested in the nuclear flood of fire and any associated issues. So I arranged for The Shalom Center to become an independent non-profit friendly to but not controlled by RRC. I continued to teach there.

In 1989, the Soviet Union began to collapse—a process that was completed by its dissolution in 1991. For the newly-independent Shalom Center, the dissolution of the Soviet Union pointed us from what we thought was now a less important planetary threat to the most important planetary threat, the climate crisis.

* * *

Through the spring of 1989, the Palestinians of the West Bank carried on what was called the *Intifada* (Arabic for "shaking off," or "Uprising.") This Intifada was almost entirely nonviolent. Official Israeli policy defined all resistance to the Occupation as terrorism. So most of the Palestinian nonviolence was met by the Israeli government with violent crackdowns.

I kept on with my commitment to support the creation of an independent Palestinian state living peacefully alongside Israel, which would have agreed to live peacefully with Palestine. It seemed to me that it was the refusal of a Palestinian state by the government of Israel which was sparking the resistance, including the few incidents of Palestinian violence. I thought that all resistance would almost disappear if there were an independent Palestine with all the tasks of governing. However, most established American Jewish organizations followed the line laid out by Israel's government. So my support for a Palestinian state became more and more difficult.

The new president of RRC, Rabbi Arthur Green, had a strong reputation, well-deserved, as an insightful scholar and excellent teacher. He had become dean of the faculty a couple years earlier. His energy, however, was not directed toward social justice as a crucial part of twentieth-century Judaism. So he seemed receptive when people became more and more hostile to my support for a Palestinian state. He called me into his office, along with Rabbi Jacob Staub, who had succeeded him as dean, and Rabbi Mordechai Liebling, who was the executive director of Reconstructionist congregations, which had a strong social-justice orientation. Green warned me that there was trouble brewing, and the four of us agreed that we might continue to meet to talk about the Israeli-Palestinian question and its implications for RRC.

Then, in July, when students had left for the summer, Green invited me to a meeting with him and Staub. There was no invitation to Mordechai Liebling this time. The meeting was not for conversation—political, personal, or institutional. Green informed me that several members of the board of governors of RRC had strongly criticized my views on Palestinian-Israeli peacemaking, had demanded that I be fired, and he agreed with them.

I went away from the meeting pretty stunned, unsure what to do. Should I protest? Quietly, inside RRC? Or loudly, to the world at large? Or simply acquiesce, leave, and take The Shalom Center with me?

Later in the summer, I went off with Phyllis to a vacation in Jamaica that had been scheduled long before. It had been offered as a gift by friends who owned a house in Negril. We had invited my brother Howard and his wife Grey to join us for a week. I sat in the shallows of the Great Atlantic talking with my brother about what to do. He encouraged me to fight. So I did.

I wrote the RRC board in protest. At least some of them were astonished. They thought President Green should have known there would be an uproar and should have let them know what he was planning. A few of them were outraged. President Emeritus Ira Silverman was a member of the board, and he resigned in protest. Leonard Fein, a leading Jewish writer and editor, who was supposed to speak at a major RRC fundraising dinner in New York, refused in protest.

I also wrote the Reconstructionist rabbis, especially since Green's letter dismissing me said I was speaking far beyond the reasonable levels of discourse among Reconstructionist rabbis. As a result, there were many letters from rabbis to Green saying they agreed with my views on a peaceful two-state solution to the conflict; and while not all Recon rabbis agreed, there was a group large enough to make them certain that I was well within a Reconstructionist viewpoint.

I also wrote to professors of Jewish Studies in universities around the country. They lived in an atmosphere of academic freedom. They were angry at my being fired for my expressed opinion. One of them was Jacob Neusner of Brown University. He wrote me that there was a simple way to stop this attack. RRC had not yet received accreditation as a rabbinical seminary and he knew many of the members of the accreditation committee. If I wrote to them, reporting I'd been fired for reasons of opinion, they'd probably suspend the accreditation process while looking into my claim. It would, he said, "ruin Artie's career."

That assertion shocked me. Art Green was not only a careful scholar but a deep one, seeking to understand what was at the root of the great Hasidic rebellion in seventeenth century Jewish life, as well as understanding the profound mystical teachings of the Hasidic rebbes. I had taken a course Green gave at RRC about the Chernobler Rebbe, a course on his book, *Tormented Master,* and could testify that at least some of the time, he was an excellent teacher. I didn't want to ruin his career.

I had prepared to file a lawsuit against the college for an unprincipled dismissal of an effective and valuable teacher. And it was very possible that indeed pursuing that course would lead to Green's career being ruined. So I decided, having made a big fuss already, to stop there and negotiate a worthy departure for The Shalom Center. I did, and the College agreed. It also politely and gently found a much more administratively calm and clever rabbi to be president. I do not know whether the circumstances of my firing led to that decision.

I know that there were many supporters of an Israeli-Palestinian two-state peace who were disappointed that I did not keep fighting. Green told many people that the issues were more complex than Israel and Palestine, but he never told me (or anyone else who told me) what those complexities were. We knew even when I was fired that there had been several times when as president of RRC, Green startled the faculty with what seemed to most of us like hysteria about some unconventional student. Those incidents and mine suggest he might have been in general worried about the impact of unconventional students or teachers on the public image and perhaps funding of RRC—but nothing more about his motives.

Now, recently, I've been asked whether I still feel I was damaged by then-President Green so long ago. I do—in one sense: I was denied the possibility of years of teaching and learning with rabbinical students. In a meeting with Green that I describe below, I mentioned that loss, and he said he was sorry for it. I continue to regret the loss, but I really did release the burden of anger. The Spirit often takes the form of unknowing.

Years after I was fired, I was present at a burial ceremony of a good mutual friend when Rabbi Brian Walt, who was leading it, said that burials should be a time of healing personal hostilities. It was then when Art Green approached me, and I think I shook hands with him as the symbol of healing the wound. But I found that my anger remained. And when I turned eighty, I found myself really wanting not to have the burden of that anger any longer. I thought, I don't want to die still carrying this burden. So I wrote to Art exactly that, and that I would like to meet.

I knew even then that "forgive" was not really the right word. I didn't know what the right word was. "Forgive" is from the German *vergeben* meaning "thoroughly give." "Giving away anger" would have been more accurate, without meaning that I had come to agree with Green's ethical choices. I wondered then, and still do now, whether carrying on the battle longer would have strengthened that wing of American Jewish thought that was prepared to criticize, as I was, the actions of an Israeli government. I think it might have, but not enough to change the history of the conflict. And if I'd held my anger tight, might it have exhausted and ruined The Shalom Center? Or exhausted and ruined me? I don't know.

There has been some deeper healing, not with Green but with RRC. It came with a very Jewish ritual twist involved. In Eastern Europe, some Jews thought that the basic allotment of life for every human was seventy years. That meant your "clock" went to zero at age seventy. And then, if you got to 83 – 70 + 13 -- you were entitled to a second bar mitzvah. I did, and I was. So in 2016, The Shalom Center gave me a bar mitzvah ceremony. I read from the Creation story—my old Torah portion. This time I understood what I was reading, and why it matters now, to the burning Earth. The RRC president, Rabbi Deborah Waxman—her own role unimaginable seventy years and seventy million years before!—asked to do the blessing for one who reads Torah. She added to the traditional blessing an announcement: In the RRC graduation of 2017, I would be awarded the College's honorary degree of Doctor of Humane Letters.

There was an audible gasp from the gathered community gathered. They knew the history. They knew what it meant. Their gasp was the Breath, the Spirit, approving.

13

The Shalom Center and Becoming ALEPH

In the traditional Lubavich Hasidic world where Reb Zalman learned Torah and life, there was a typical practice for hierarchical teaching and learning: On the eve of Shabbat or a holy day, the rebbe would gather his male disciples (*Hasidim*) at a *tisch* (table). The rebbe would sit in an especially sumptuous chair and teach Torah at least half the night.

Reb Zalman transformed this practice. Men, women, people of all sorts, orientations, and genders would cluster around the tisch. Zalman would sit in the special chair, teaching Torah for about twenty minutes. Then he would stand and ask everyone to move one chair to the left. And he would also move one chair to the left. He told everyone to sit down in their new chair, and he would sit in an ordinary chair, relinquishing the rebbe's special chair. Then he would speak to whoever was now sitting in the rebbe's chair: "Look deep into yourself. Find there the rebbe-spark within you. Nurture it as you would nurture a candle-spark into a flame. When you are clear and the flame is clear, teach the Torah you have discovered within you to the community."

After about twenty minutes, he would again call on all of us to move one chair to the left. And the process would keep on.

In this way he would treat the rebbe-spark as equally potent and potential in every member of the community. But not, he said, like an arithmetical flood of equal check-marks, like the votes of people in a voting booth. In each of us the rebbe-spark would glow uniquely. We would all teach something deep and new, we would all learn many things that were deep and new.

* * *

In January 1991, the U.S. government under the first President Bush went to war against Iraq after its government invaded and overwhelmed Kuwait. To protect one sovereign state against the predatory attacks of another was the official justification for the U.S. invasion. Another reason often cited by opponents of the war was stabilizing and controlling the flow of oil to the U.S. and other major industrial nations.

Might the war spread? This possibility worried Reb Zalman. He felt a special spiritual call to prevent or limit war because he himself had been an immediate victim of World War II. With his family he'd fled Vienna as Nazi Germany accomplished its *Anschluss* (annexation) of Austria. He ended up living under near-prison conditions imposed by the pro-Nazi, anti-Jewish Vichy regime in southern France. So Reb Zalman turned to ancient Jewish tradition to resist a wider war.

Long ago, Jews chose when they were facing the calamities of drought, or plague, or famine, or war, to call the community to fast. This tradition had been shaped into a liturgy for calling such a fast as it is described in *Mishnah Ta'anit* (Chapters 1-3) of the Talmud. Zalman called his most intimate community—P'nai Or in Philadelphia, for whom he was the local as well as the national rabbi—to gather in Washington, DC to call for a communal fast to end the war. We did, carrying out the ritual with a Torah scroll. And the war ended on Purim night, a night of festive celebration for Jews everywhere. President Bush stopped short of a full occupation, which prevented an utter calamity. (The calamity did happen a decade later, when his son as president decided to outdo him.)

* * *

During the early 1990s when Reb Zalman still lived in Philadelphia, we used once a week to walk together around a track at a nearby neighborhood high school. One of those mornings, he turned to me and said, "*Du bist a gonif.*" You are a thief. Astonished, I replied, "What do you mean?" He said, "You robbed from me the chance to make you a rabbi!"

So I kept thinking as we kept walking. Then said, "Ok, it's been ten years of learning on my own since you first tried. I think I'm ready to learn with the guidance of a *beit din* (rabbinical court). I'd like you to be chair. And I'd like to ask some others from the different branches of Judaism." "Ok!" he said.

So I started asking. I asked Rabbi Max Ticktin, my beloved friend in Washington, a graduate of the Conservative seminary. I asked Rabbi Laura Geller, a Reform rabbi in Los Angeles and an early Jewish feminist, strongly committed to social-justice activism. They both said yes. I asked Dr. Judith Plaskow, the preeminent Jewish feminist theologian. She demurred. "Arthur, you know I'm not a rabbi. How can someone who is not a rabbi ordain a rabbi?" I answered, "First of all, Judith, three rabbis of different origins have said yes, so that's a kosher rabbinical court I'm asking you to join. But more important, I don't want to join the rabbinate as it is; I want to join a midrash on the rabbinate, and you are the midrash that I want." "It still feels strange, but all right, I'll do it," said Judith.

So for five years I read what they said to read and did what they said to do. Then Zalman said he thought I was ready. I said, "I think so, too."

Zalman suggested that our "seminary without walls" be capped and completed by having the ceremony in our living room, so people from the Mt. Airy community in Philadelphia could easily come. And on the morning before, he said he'd like to go to a nearby non-Orthodox *mikveh* (ritual bath for sacred immersion]. My son, David, who had come from Washington, DC for the ceremony, said he'd like to come too. So we three appeared at the mikveh. As we prepared for the first of three total immersions, Zalman recited the lineage of his own ordination back to the Ba'al Shem Tov, founder of Hasidism. David said, "In that case, I'd like to dedicate the second immersion to the lineage of the future. We left the third one to the Spirit.

Back in our living room, with about thirty other people, we especially welcomed the beit din rabbis Zalman and Max Ticktin, plus Judith Plaskow in the room, and Rabbi Geller by phone from California. They did *smikha*—that is, "leaning" their hands on my head and shoulders to say the sacred words of transmission. Then Zalman asked me whether I had anything to say.

I stumbled and fumbled to say, "Until now I thought I had become a reasonably knowledgeable American Jew. Now I feel like an unknowledgeable rabbi." To which my friend, neighbor, former student, always teacher and co-activist Rabbi Mordechai Liebling called out: "Arthur, that's how we all know you are now a rabbi! Rabbis are people who know enough of Judaism to know how much we don't know!" The community fragmented into tears, laughter, mazel tovs, wisps of the Spirit in the air. I was no longer a *gonif*.

* * *

Phyllis and I were sitting near the departure gate in the airport in Geneva enroute back home to Philadelphia after a week-long interfaith conference that had brought together religious leaders/scholars from around the world. It was one of many we attended abroad (Geneva, Madrid, Vienna, Upsala, Delhi) and within the U.S.

At these gatherings, in general, the format was always the same: talking heads sharing their intellectual prowess. We had met some very bright, even interesting people from many different religions and countries, but as we sat waiting to board our plane, we realized that we didn't care if we ever saw any of these people again. Not because they all weren't nice, not because we weren't social and caring, but because in the interfaith conference "rules of the game," we engaged with one another ONLY in the intellectual arena: I showed you mine, and you showed me yours. There was no touching.

In contrast were the many retreats we've been part of as

participants or organizers modeled by our teacher, Rabbi Zalman Schachter Shalomi, in which all of his teachings included experiences in the Four Worlds of Kabbalah: *Assiya* (physical reality), *Yetzira* (emotional reality), *Bria* (intellectual, creative reality), *Atzilut* (spiritual reality). So Phyllis and I began to imagine an annual gathering over Memorial Day weekend of the Tent of Abraham, Hagar, and Sarah, as an interfaith retreat of women and men of a range of ages coming together at a retreat center to put the Four Worlds model into operation.

We began our Tent each year by inviting everyone to share a "brief" version of their spiritual journey that had brought them to this moment of integration as people committed to action, to relationship with others, to knowledge, and to spirit. Though many of the same people came each year, we found that those stories changed from year to year with new experiences and new ways of seeing and understanding what came before. These stories always touched and resonated with one another. It didn't matter in a short time in which "door" we made our connection with whatever we called G!d; by the end of the first day, we could see and feel our connections with one another in real and intimate ways.

With that as our entry point, the meal times we shared, the bedrooms we shared with a roommate from another mother, and our openness to try on practices and thoughts different from the ones we were most familiar with grew exponentially at the retreat and in our lives afterwards.

Because we met over a three-day weekend, we asked people to commit to being together for the entire retreat. On Fridays, we asked our Muslim brothers and sisters to lead us in prayer that we could all participate in; on Saturdays we asked our Jewish sisters and brothers to do the same; on Sunday we asked our Christian sisters and brothers to do the same.

Asking a religious leader to create a prayer experience both authentic to their religion and also permissible for those of other religions to enter into as full participants is complex, especially to leaders who haven't done so before. After the first year, we found it was better for the leader not to be ordained and somewhat freer to include others out of their own experience of being excluded. Not surprisingly, the women in our group were generally more adept at making those translations because they had felt themselves left out of religions' leadership at some point in history or even currently. From the start, women shared that as a common bond.

Listening to one another find the "religious home" to belong to, often different from the one we were born into, rang a bell for many. Even when our choices were different, there was something we all recognized about the search for belonging. Being able to do holy scripture study together, chant together, do Zikr, or sit silently in meditation made us all feel welcome inside the experience rather than looking on from the outside as at a foreign object. Our personal spiritual storytelling mostly opened us up to praying and studying together and meditating together without resistance or fear.

Toward the end of each retreat, we agreed on an action we might take in the places where we lived in order to move the arc a little closer to justice. Some of those actions intensified our lifelong connections.

How different all this was from that day years earlier at the Geneva airport when there had been no intimacy created at the interfaith conference and it didn't matter if we ever saw each other again!

* * *

As the Jewish Renewal network that Zalman had seeded flourished and flowered, he talked more and more about "deep ecumenism." That meant uncovering the deep shared values and hopes of different religions. Each, he suggested, had its own ecologic niche, intended to serve the universal good. Like the heart and the liver in a single body, each and all bore a shared DNA to help the bearer live. That sharing was what deep ecumenism celebrated.

I was at one such learning when someone new asked, "But it seems to me there is a real problem with Christianity. We claim the Messiah has not yet come, they claim he has. How do you make deep ecumenism out of that?" Zalman said, "When she comes, we will ask her whether it's the first or second time."

There was a burst of laughter from the assembled learners. But, I thought, the joke is already deep—something about humor being at the heart of it all. If the Spirit can't laugh, what's the point? Here, the joke is that although the liver and the heart and the brain seem so different, they all unfold from and preserve the same DNA, to keep the body they share thriving. Zalman was saying that no one religious claim is the point. What both religions yearn for is the messianic age of peace and justice. "Messiah"—a specific person—is just a cover story.

"There are no true or false Messiahs," Zalman would say. "Each one is an experiment."

* * *

In 1970, Channel 13 in New York City—a public-oriented TV station—decided that Jewish mysticism was a growing edge of New York's creativity. They invited five Jews who were reaching toward something maybe mystical to have a conversation on camera. The five were two from the Lubavitch community; Herbert Weiner, a Reform rabbi and author of a book titled *9 ½ Mystics* about the old/new turn in Judaism; Rabbi Shlomo Carlebach, a former shining Lubavitch teacher who had left his nurturing place and brought his magic song-writing and singing to reach out to young and spiritually thirsty Jews; and me, the recent author of *The Freedom Seder* and till then a secular progressive activist. The invitation seemed to promise an exciting conversation and an open-minded audience; so I said yes.

When we converged on the TV studio, there was a troubling detail: The Lubavitchers insisted they could sit at the same table with the Reform rabbi who had been nice to them in a book, but not with a renegade and heretic. So they insisted on two tables: one for Shlomo and me, one for the two of them. Weiner could move back and forth. This act of contempt and disconnection rankled, but the attractions of reaching a New York City audience won out. So Shlomo and I stayed. I was not yet comfortable with language of the Spirit, so I didn't inquire beyond my own feelings. And I figured the encounter was over and done.

But thirty years later, I was invited to speak in Milwaukee. My friend Max Samson, who had arranged some of my visit, asked if I'd like to meet the local rabbi of a Lubavitcher shul for lunch. I said sure, and we met at a kosher restaurant. We had a pleasant talk, and then the Lubavitcher rabbi said, "One of our constant values has been friendship toward all Jews."

"Weeeell," I said. And I told the story of Channel 13 and the two tables.

He turned so pale it would be more honest to call it green. He said, "I was there. Sort-of there, anyway. I was very young, just a teen. All of 770 Eastern Parkway [Lubavitch headquarters] was so excited by the invitation to speak to a big audience that I bummed a ride in the auto the two stars took to Channel 13."

Long pause. "We were wrong. Sometimes we made mistakes. I'm sorry."

We all sat quietly. I was thinking, change? What about women? What about Palestinians? What about beating swords into plow shares? Still, I reached out a hand to accept the apology. He took it. Now I knew What / Who the Spirit was / is / will be. She / He / They didn't roll over in joy at this *teshuvah*—repentance—but I could feel a slow headshake.

* * *

In 2011, just recovering from a throat cancer with a very scratchy voice, I was surprised by an invitation from the alumni association of my high school. Sixty-one years after I graduated, what did they want? They were inviting me to join a special honor group of alumni. There was a perk: I would get to give a six-minute speech to the assembly of the whole student body. I would be one of six who did this. The idea seemed to be that by parading a police chief alumnus, a corporate-boss alumnus, a TV star singer alumna, an alumna who was chief of nursing at Johns Hopkins University, they could convince the students that if they paid attention in class or an assembly, they could make it in the world.

But me? A rabbi whose main work in the world was asking questions and advocating for justice? Still, the perk sounded interesting. What would it feel like, speaking six decades later to an assembly of students that I remembered so well? So Phyllis drove me to Baltimore. It was easy to point out the school. It had been built more than a century ago to look like a castle on the hill, and it still did. "No change at all," I told Phyllis.

But when we got inside, enormous change. In 1950, the students were all white and all boys. Now about sixty percent of them were Black or brown, and about sixty percent of them were women. And at the assembly where we were about to speak, there was a jazz orchestra and no hymn.

Luckily, I was the last of the six to speak. I started by pointing out the differences between 1950 and now. Then I told the story of myself as editor, the absurdity of a network of *future* teachers' clubs that were segregated, and the gentlemanly vice-principal who told me that not in his lifetime or in mine would segregation in the Baltimore public schools be ended. "And in 1954," I said to the assembly, "the Baltimore public schools were peacefully desegregated. The vice-principal was still alive and so was I. How did that happen? Your parents changed America!"

There was long applause. Then I took a deep breath and started the part of my speech that was the real point. "Suppose a pleasant and respected head of an oil company comes to speak to you: 'Even if everybody knows that burning oil is wrecking planet Earth, in my lifetime and in yours, America will not stop burning oil.' You listen and then you tell him, 'We will change America!' And suppose some bossy bishop comes here and says to you, 'In my lifetime and yours, we will not allow gay people to serve in the army or as foster parents.' Say to him, 'We will change America!'"

I said a couple more like that. And then I said, "If some senator says to you, 'In my lifetime and yours, we will not ensure that everyone has decent medical care as a human right.' What will you say to him?" And 1,000 kids roared back at me, *"We will change America!"*

If just ten of those kids keep that commitment in their minds and hearts and bellies... thank you, Spirit.

※ ※ ※

I think it was 2013 when Zalman focused his annual address to Ohalah (the organization of Jewish Renewal clergy) on his sexual adventures earlier in life, his sense now that the experiments may not have been as holy as he thought they were then, and an apology to anyone who felt then or still feels discomfort at the possibility of his having used spiritual leadership in illegitimate ways. When he finished, there was a stunned silence.

I stood up and said: "Reb Zalman, as you know, I do not really like the traditional practice of standing when a teacher enters or leaves the room. But when a teacher teaches in an unusually profound way, I feel moved to stand in deep respect for that teaching. Today I feel moved to stand to honor your extraordinary teaching this morning." And I stayed standing.

Around the room, a few people stood with me. Then more. Soon, everyone. In silence, till he left the room.

Notice, my statement was "I"—not a directive that the *Kahal* (the entire group) should stand. Indeed, by mentioning my own distaste for the traditional practice, I think I was giving permission to anyone to not stand. (I didn't work this all out on the spot; I just did what felt right, and I am thinking it through right now, writing you.) And I'm not claiming that I always get it right—even what I myself would call "right," let alone what others would.

※ ※ ※

At the brownstone in New York where I met Gloria Steinem for the second time in fifty-five years, we talked about what it meant to be elders, almost eighty, and still activists.

The Shalom Center was already planning to celebrate my eightieth birthday with a gathering intended to raise both money and political consciousness. When we realized that she too was almost eighty and still a committed activist, I invited her to join me in the celebration and bring her insights on America and how it was doing. She said yes.

So in the fall of 2013 we arranged for a wonderful interviewer and therapist, Dr. Dan Gottlieb, to interview each one of us separately, asking what it feels like to be an activist at this age. One of the questions he asked Gloria was, "What's your sense of America and what is it like to be eighty and still trying to fight for the rights of women?" She answered, "America, the whole country, is like a woman who has just walked out of an abusive marriage. It's the most liberating moment and the most dangerous moment in her life. Her abusive husband may be so furious as to kill her. Either there is a community ready to receive and protect her or she is in really great danger. We are all like that now."

This is a moment I never forgot. The first time I met Gloria, in 1968, it seemed such a casual meeting that I never even remembered it. This one I never forgot. She took her experience in the feminist struggle and turned it into a universal message of danger and possibility, possible transformation.

We didn't know then that three years later, in 2016, a non-fictional, non-metaphorical, real abusive man—who makes abusing women something to brag about—would be elected president of the United States. And he was ready to abuse and to kill more than uppity women. Gloria's metaphor for the whole country became the reality of our country.

It still is. The denial of women's constitutional right to control their own bodies, is only a piece of the broader attack on women. And even the growing attack on—what's next, the right to choose birth control?—is only a piece of the attack from the right-wing part of the country on all who walked out of the abusive house of exclusive "democracy."

A century ago, exclusive democracy in America was limited to white Christian males. What we have lived through in the 1960s, '70s, and '80s was a challenge toward an inclusive democracy. There has now emerged a group of people who want to make what they remember as the whole of political leadership in "their" America, into the whole leadership of an America where there are many communities searching for a role in political leadership. They intend to do this by enforcing a white, heterosexual, male Christian nationalism that treats all other communities as third class citizens. Black people, brown people, women, all the flavors of the LGBTQ+ communities, Jews, Muslims, indigenous Americans, all challenge the notion of that America. All these communities won a lot of second-level power that they didn't have before. Those past decades were a moment of possible transformation and real danger.

There had to be communities ready to welcome those of us who walked out of the old abusive house. There had to be people to receive and multiply the challenge. There have been many, but maybe not enough. Still trembling on the edge: Pharaoh's army (under the modern label, "fascism") behind us, and the Unknown ahead. Gloria's metaphor was the truth about where we were. Where we still are.

* * *

Early in 1993, there were two radically Jewish organizations. One was P'nai Or, focused on new liturgy rooted in Torah that would enhance personal spiritual growth. The other was The Shalom Center, focused on new liturgy rooted in Torah that would enhance activism for justice and for love and healing between *Adamah* (Earth) and *adam* (human earthlings). Both were stirring great interest in the Jewish community, and both were in serious financial trouble. Both had their lead offices in the Mt. Airy neighborhood of Philadelphia.

I led The Shalom Center and also co-edited *New Menorah*, P'nai Or's national magazine. I went to Reb Zalman, who led P'nai Or, and said: "You often teach that we, all of us, are great at creative ideas and projects, and not so great at funding them. You know that I care a lot about personal spiritual growth, and I know that you care a lot about preventing war, pursuing justice, and responding to Earth's *schrei* [Yiddish, "scream"]—outcry of pain as the climate crisis worsens."

I continued, "I have a strong hunch that Rabbi Rachel Cowan, who is head of grant-making on Jewish programs at the Nathan Cummings Foundation, would be emotionally and intellectually excited and financially generous if P'nai Or and The Shalom Center were to merge."

Zalman said, "Yes! Let's do it!"

And so we did. And Rachel did. We worked on a new name for our merged organization. We started discussing "Alliance for Jewish Renewal" and one of us—I'm not sure who—said "'Alliance for,' that sounds like *ALEPH!*" Others said, "First letter of the Hebrew *aleph-bet,* so lots of untutored Jews know it; first letter of the Ten Utterances at Sinai, so it has deep meaning for lots of learned Jewish mystics!" And we could all feel the Spirit rejoicing.

* * *

April 4th is the *yahrzeit* (death anniversary) of Dr. Martin Luther King, Jr., who was murdered on April 4, 1968. And it was April 4, 1967, exactly one year before his death, when Dr. King gave probably his greatest speech, called "Beyond Vietnam: A Time to Break the Silence." The speech took on the gravely heavy message of opposing the U.S. war against Vietnam and calling for its urgent, immediate end.

And it went further—"beyond Vietnam." King said that "racism, materialism, and militarism" were the giant triplets afflicting not only American politics and culture but afflicting our soul. He warned that there would be no way to annul these triplets without a revolution of values. He talked of "the fierce urgency of now."

Why did Dr. King (or the ghost draftsman of the speech, Vincent Harding) use "triplet" instead of "trio, triad," or even simply "three"? They never said, but what occurs to me is that biological triplets share DNA, unlike the others. They are of the same family. The DNA they share is a wish to dominate, to subjugate, rooted in greed for more. More wealth, more power, more ability to kill more people: the ultimate in subjugation. So I once asked Brother Vincent—he was a pastor, a scholar, a historian, PhD, and author—whether "materialism" in the triplets was a code word for "capitalism." He responded hesitantly: "I think not. Brother Martin wanted to talk not only about a social system in the almost-abstract, but about the close-in lived experience of a person, a family."

There are some who still think that when Dr. King gave this speech, he signed his death warrant. Could those who had real power in America allow such ideas to be given public words by a public prophet?

In my own life, April 4th turned out to be a turning point to an expanded vision of myself, of America, of the world. On April 4, 1969 we held the first Freedom Seder, a Passover ritual that for the first time in history included a freedom struggle other than the ancient Israelite struggle—a story I told in Chapter 6. We included heroic figures in the ongoing freedom struggle of Black Americans: from Nat Turner, enslaved but rebellious, to Eldridge Cleaver, a rebellious Black Panther who welcomed the Jewish people as an ally. We included Gandhi and Thoreau and Fannie Lou Hamer, the rebellious share-cropper who led the Mississippi Freedom Democratic Party.

April 4 was a sacred, holy day.

All that was on my mind in 2024 as the telephone rang. It was an influential member of the board of ALEPH: Alliance for Jewish Renewal. That was an organization I co-founded; but then I had been pushed aside when I actively campaigned for one of the planks of the ALEPH platform: support for self-determination for the children of Hagar and Sarah, sons fathered by Abraham. That is, in modern terms, a new state of Palestine living peacefully alongside Israel.

The ALEPH board member who called me on April 4, 2024, said she was on a mission of reconciliation. She asked whether I would be willing on July 28 of that year to speak as a "living prophet." Then she paused. "For five minutes," she said.

My guts were yanked in several directions at once. I would be pleased to have some public moment of reconciliation with ALEPH. The notion of being labeled a "living prophet" jarred me. Dr. King was a real living prophet, able to stand with Isaiah and Jeremiah. Who was I to wear that label? And the proof that it was almost laughable was the suggestion of five minutes for the resident living prophet to speak. Try telling that to Amos!

So Dr. King's yahrzeit and the offer of such a title even for just five minutes, clanged against each other. I said I could make the date, but I would have to think a lot about everything that was involved.

Meanwhile, something truly weird happened. My left shoulder had for months twinged with mild discomfort from a torn rotator cuff. But then, suddenly in mid-conversation, it flared up with intense pain. Only hours afterward did I ask myself why. Was it the grief for Dr. King and the world gone so badly without him? Or was it pain for the fusion of honor and insult wrapped up in an invitation to speak as a prophet for five minutes? It took a couple days for me to ask myself: what if it's both? What if my body is telling me it's being wrenched into pain by the calculus of praise and ridicule?

I told the emissary, "Thanks, but no. I would be glad to join in an act of reconciliation—but only if it were serious."

14
Sages of All Ages

Sometime after Nixon bombed Haiphong Harbor, a delegation of American clergy went to Europe with the desperate hope of somehow mobilizing Europeans to oppose the U.S. war so strenuously as to force it to end. They visited the Vatican and met with a high-ranking cardinal. All of them said their piece except for Rabbi Leonard Beerman. So the cardinal turned to Leonard and said, "Rabbi, I realize that you have not spoken."

Leonard said, "I have been sitting here thinking about the level of criticism that has been coming to the Church in our generation as a result of what some have thought was its weakness in responding to Nazism and to the oppression of the Jews, even before the mass annihilations and even then. I hope that a generation from now, the Church will not have acted in such a way in regard to Vietnam that there will need to be directed at the Church criticism of its failure to act against the war in Vietnam."

What the cardinal then did, no one told me.

* * *

One of the remarkable people in Washington, DC in the 1960s and '70s was Izzy Stone—more formally, I.F. Stone. He was one of the great radical journalists of all American history. He covered the establishment of the State of Israel, the McCarthyist attack on the left and many liberals, the benign explosion of the civil rights movement, the war in Vietnam and the anti-war movement, all of them calling forth his commitment to justice, peace, and above all truth.

One day I was having lunch with Izzy. He said to me, "They start out by calling you heretic and traitor; if you stick to the truth long enough, they start calling you a saint. Then you are really dead. Don't let them call you a saint, and keep telling the truth anyway."

* * *

Late in 1970, Mike Taber came to me with a project. He was the founder of Jews for Urban Justice, a radical group of young Jews who had taken on the holy work of organizing the Freedom Seder, and we were able to build a friendship. He said, "I'm never sure who we are, and I'd like to have a stronger sense of where we come from, given the various Jewish communities. I'd like to visit three places in New York: the purely ethnic nostalgia of the soda they call the two cents plain; the central committee of the *Yiddisher Arbeiter-Bund*; and Rabbi Heschel." I said, "Fine!" and we set up a date and times for the meetings.

We went to the drug store where they invented the two cents plain. Didn't move me much. Then we visited a gathering of the central committee of the Bund in Eastern Europe. They had been a powerful political party, socialist, taking an important part in the revolutionary efforts against the tsar, uninterested or opposed to religious Judaism, and opposed to Zionism. We knocked on the door of their meeting and were cordially welcomed. We asked the chair of the meeting whether they had received the items of literature, liturgy, newsletters, etc. that emerged from our work in Washington. That included a copy of *The Freedom Seder*. He looked in his briefcase, pulled out the copy we had sent, and waved it in the air.

"I like, we all like, the politics of your haggadah," he said. "But," he continued, "vhy, vhy! did you keep God in de haggadah?" His voice rose as he kept talking. "I vent to yeshiva, I became a shoshalist, and then the rabbis burned our books, our Bundist calls to the people to rise up. And you vould keep God in this haggadah? Vhat kind of shoshalism is that?"

Next, we swiftly made our way to Rabbi Heschel in his office at the Jewish Theological Seminary. He greeted us cordially and asked, "Who else have you seen today in New York? I hope you didn't come all this way from Washington just to see me."

We told him about the Bund, about how angry they still were more than fifty years later, about religion, and how everyone on their central committee seemed to be more than eighty years old. Heschel looked sad. "I love the Bund," he said. "At Vilna where I was studying Talmud all day, I went at night to learn from the Bund. It saddens me that I am not surprised that they seem to have no younger generation. I think that any group or organization that totally cuts itself off from Torah may have a momentary impact on Jewish thought and action, but not a continuing presence."

We asked Rabbi Heschel the same question we asked the Bund. "Did you get the literature we sent you, and if you did, what did you think?"

"It was all very interesting. I enjoyed *The Freedom Seder* very much. I was intrigued by your seder for Shabbat, a liturgy to explain at a Friday evening meal what Shabbat is all about. And I was honored by your using so many passages from me in my book *The Sabbath* as explanations of various aspects of Shabbat." He continued, "I am not sure whether after three thousand years the Jewish people actually still need a haggadah, a seder, for Shabbat. But perhaps the decline in spiritual experience has been so great among the many American Jews that it would be valuable."

Then. "But there is one thing you sent that troubled me a great deal." We shuddered our way into very close attention. "You sent your periodic newsletter. The content seemed exciting. But its title!—yes, its title! That's what troubled me. You named it the 'Jewish Urban Guerilla.' Well, if you were really urban guerillas..." His voice trailed off. "But you are not. What weapons do we have?" I remember being struck that this wise and learned rabbi was using "we" to include us.

"What weapons do we have? We do not have guns. We do not have much money. We only have words as our weapons. We must use our words by aiming them as precisely as we would, God forbid, if we had guns." Then he stopped talking, and just looked at us.

We told him we would go back and discuss the name of the newsletter with our comrades. We did, and we ended up with some boring name. Boring but accurate.

The teaching for me was very powerful. Later I learned that Heschel himself in creating his wonderful books would write only five or six words a day that he would keep. He would write, think about the sentence, and almost always throw it away in some companion's waste basket, the first several versions of his draft. Only then would the writing begin to become real.

* * *

We usually think of "sages" as older people who have learned some wisdom and then give it over. But I am especially interested in the sagacious insights of young people, because they seem readier than elders to break loose of "official" or conventional understandings of the world. Indeed, I've tried to listen closely to the last words of the last of the classical Hebrew prophets, Malachi:

> I [YHWH, the Breath of Life,] will send Elijah the Prophet to turn the hearts of parents to their children and the hearts of children to their parents, lest I come [as a hurricane of change] and destroy all Earth.

I assume that Malachi was using "parents" and "children" as a poetic reference to "elders" and "youth."

Young people have shifted my way of understanding Torah and the world. When we are open to their wonderings and ask them open questions without "right answers," they can share tremendous wisdom. Over the years, I've learned from the Spirit shining through my own children and grandchildren, from the kids I taught in our cooperative Sunday school (the Fabrangen *Cheder*), from the children of my friends, and from the stories of wisdom from youth that others have shared. I learned from children and teenagers:

- Deeply experiencing embodied ritual can provide insights into how to connect to the Divine.
- We can find new interpretations of our texts by reading carefully and asking what the words really mean.
- We can gain understanding of Torah stories by imagining the actual appearance of the objects and people described.
- Shifting our prayer language to include non-male language for God (She, They) can bring new opportunities to connect to the Spirit.
- While each individual life contains a spark of divinity, it is only when we are clear that we're all connected together do we truly become the image of God.
- Learning and talking (about God, prayer, Torah, and Talmud) is only one way of bringing Divine Spirit to the world; serving and caring for others and their psyches and bodies is also a spiritual practice.
- A serious pursuit of traditional commentators like Rashi can, if brought to address new realities, bring life-affirming results.

All these convinced me: the generations which follow mine are bringing light to our world as they learn and live.

"You do not need to finish the work," said Rabbi Tarfon in the Talmud—perhaps because he knew that coming generations would pursue it. But, he added, "Don't quit!"—perhaps because he knew elders' creativity can help grow these seeds! Those who try to stamp out fresh ideas because they trouble the power-holders will find themselves stamping out the communities they're trying to preserve.

15
God and Earth

In 1971, the Breath of Life breathed the first hint that became my more-and-more connection to the neighborhood of Mount Airy. I was invited to speak on "Jewish radicalism" at the Germantown Jewish Centre. Even the title of my talk stirred up excitement and annoyance, among other Jews who thought they were the "radical Jews" of Philadelphia. So I ended up offering them some time and space on the synagogue's public stage where I was to speak. We made ourselves a community instead of a warring bunch of rock stars.

I was invited because the rabbi of the synagogue, Elias Charry, was an explorer. A week or two after the synagogue schedule announced me, it announced that Jane Fonda was going to speak. Most of the country thought she was a traitor. She had gone for a friendly visit to North Vietnam in the midst of the U.S. war against North and South Vietnam. So if I was an *enfant terrible* in the Jewish world because I'd written *The Freedom Seder*, suddenly the Germantown Jewish Centre was ready to host people who were making trouble.

I was invited to dinner at the rabbi's house—and when I got there many of the leaders of the congregation were also there for dinner. One was missing. He was an environmental lawyer for the city of Philadelphia and somehow had been the key person in suggesting they invite me. For him, to be late was shocking.

When he got there, he was clearly exhausted. We asked him what happened and he said that some factory high on the Schuylkill River had turned a knob in the wrong direction and released thousands of gallons of oil-impregnated water into the Philadelphia water supply. So he had spent hours organizing the legal system and the engineers to put a plug in the main lines to turn the water aside so it would not enter the Philadelphia system.

His ordeal and its political meaning was in my head and heart as we entered the synagogue. The Conservative *shul*/synagogue included in the recitation of the Sh'ma, a central prayer in most services, the traditional second paragraph, even though most progressive shuls took it out. That paragraph said that how humans acted made a big difference to rain and wind and ocean and abundance. I was blown away. It was totally new to me.

So I got up and I said, "I was invited to talk about Jewish radicalism and I didn't know what I was going to say—but let me read you a passage of Jewish radicalism." And I read the second paragraph of the Sh'ma. "Take it seriously: what we do has an effect on the natural world."

The Spirit applauded, but most of the Jewish community didn't pay attention. I found for the next four decades or so it was really hard to convince Jews that issues about Earth were serious Jewish issues. But I realized there was a praiseworthy reason for that. When Jews were thrown out of the Land of Israel, and then from many other lands, they could never make an emotional, let alone a physical or political, connection with Earth. What they focused on was trying to make a decent Jewish community within the *shtetl* (a Jewish neighborhood particularly in Eastern Europe) or wherever they were. With the entry of many Jews to full citizenship in parts of Europe or the U.S., they carried concern for the social good as a Jewish value to the whole society. Justice, yes! Peace, yes! Earth? A distraction.

It took many years to persuade the Jewish community that Earth was a legitimate Jewish issue. That not only were we facing a planetary crisis, but the Hebrew Bible is a treasury of forgotten wisdom about nurturing Earth.

Some early Zionists were more interested in reconnecting with Earth and its rhythmic rest than they were in a State. But modern Israel has been influenced by modern economics. That meant coal and oil. Up to a point it worked, and we only began to discover it didn't work in the 1970s. Meanwhile, Big Oil and Big Coal were investing their hyper-wealth in making more political power. Could the Hebrew Bible win a struggle with them? Could the Spirit, the *Ruach*, the Breath, the Wind?

* * *

One night in early March 1972, I came home from a Fabrangen meeting feeling far more exhausted than any meeting could have made me. As I fell into bed, I realized that my elbow was sore, with a red patch. A boil, I thought. I tried to fall asleep.

Four hours later, there was a red streak up my arm and my temperature was 105. I called my doctor. "That's blood poisoning," he said, his voice tense and brittle. "I'll call an all-night drugstore. Get hold of penicillin. Right now!"

For three days, I took huge doses of aspirin and penicillin. On the fourth night, I couldn't sleep at all. Every time I closed my eyes, a color movie began to unreel: places I had been, people I'd known. My life was running like a film before my eyes.

That film ran all the way into the present. Then a sequence from the future started. I watched myself give a sermon at a synagogue where I was due to speak in a week. And I listened to the discussion after my talk. I was asked a question: "After your experience with the Freedom Seder, how do you feel about writing liturgies?" And I answered: "There is only one more that I would like to do: a memorial that connects the Holocaust and Hiroshima." "Then why don't you write it?" "I can't! Not yet, anyway. I'm working on it."

Suddenly, not in the film of my future but in my most immediate present, my arm began to throb and burn as if some unimaginable heat from Hiroshima and Auschwitz were seething in it, trying to drip down through fingers that could not write it out. Then there welled up in me a total certainty, clear as a voice but without even the semblance of a sound, a total certainty in every vein and muscle, in every nerve and bone. It said: "If you, if anyone, can ever write the liturgy that connects their suffering, those very dead will live again. Their bones will join again, one to the other; their ashes will turn to flesh again; the breath of life will fill their lungs again."

Sweat poured out from every inch of me, my arm stopped burning, I touched my forehead to find it cool. And I fell asleep.

A week later, my doctor told me that before penicillin, people died from blood poisoning. He said it used to take four days. At that burning moment on the fourth night, I would have been dying.

Two years later, I bumped into a passage of Jeremiah: "Your words burn like a fever in my bones. If I shut the doors of my mouth to keep Your word within me, turn all my strength toward keeping silent— still, I cannot stop my burning tongue." I gasped. For an instant, my body flamed again, the words that had burned their way into my arm came back again and I relived the quandary of that painful night: what could it possibly mean to write a liturgy for the Holocaust and Hiroshima? A real liturgy, not just a piece of paper but a "people's work," as the Greek of "liturgy" means.

No answers came.

Then I told this story to a friend of mine, and he arranged for me to have lunch with Elie Wiesel, who listened and said only: "If you keep telling the story, its heat will dissipate. If you want to do what you heard to do, keep the story within you." Did I really believe those dead would breathe again if I could write the liturgy—an echo of Ezekiel's dry bones? No. Did I really believe Wiesel's advice that if I told other people the story it would wither away in my telling? No. Then what did I believe? What was the Spirit trying to teach me?

First, that like Jeremiah, I believed the fever in my body was trying to tell me about fire in the world. The fires of the past. But more importantly, the Fire of the future.

It took years of thought and action, dreams of Spirit, to learn a crucial midrash: Abraham accosting God, as Abe stared at the fires consuming Sodom. He could not see beyond the city, so he thought the whole world was burning. He accused God of betraying their promise after the flood never to destroy the whole world again. "Oh! You did not promise there would be no flood of fire, only none of water."

Could that be the meaning of the fire in my body? That I must act against the future flood of fire? By 1983—more than ten years later—I was teaching at the Reconstructionist Rabbinical College and founding The Shalom Center to speak a Jewish voice about the bomb. By then, Carl Sagan and a myriad of scientists were teaching that the fire of just 100 H-bombs could smother Earth in enough dust from every incinerated major city that photosynthesis would stop and life would end. I also knew from my work on solar-energy co-ops: burning limitless fossil fuels would choke the planetary Breath of Life. It would exhale so much CO_2 that the heat-trapping gas would scorch, then burn, then broil the Earth we share.

Either way, the flood of fire. My arm, my body, a fever in my bones to model planetary fire. I wrote *Between the Fires* to engage the Spirit in proclaiming truth.

※ ※ ※

In the mid-1970s, a few people began to know and say that the carbon-based economy was endangering the planet. There were two places that knowledge was crucial—inside Big Oil—especially Exxon—and inside Big Politics—the presidential administration of Jimmy Carter.

Carter took the warnings from ecologists and others seriously enough to put solar collectors on the roof of the White House—not really for their own sake, but to make a political statement throughout the country. And he placed some progressive social activists from local politics in Washington, DC, in a newly sensitive office on community grass-roots energy in the Department of Energy. Key people there were Tina Hobson and Rev. Channing Phillips, whom I knew well from my civil rights activism and from the DNC in Chicago in 1968. (I refer you back to Chapter 8.)

In 1978, I was working with a skilled and creative physicist, Dr. Leonard Rodberg, to explore whether America's need for energy could be produced in a more democratic way—not by Big Oil and Big Coal but by new community-based technology that would bypass producing the heat-trapping gas of carbon dioxide. After some initial explorations in Black and white neighborhoods in DC, we submitted a grant proposal to the Carter Department of Energy, to explore the possibility of community-based production of solar energy. The grant was provided and we produced a convincing report: community organizing to produce solar energy could win community support. Our report was a handbook for how community activists could do it.

It was so convincing that in mid-1980 we asked for and received a contract to make the handbook real: to organize an activist campaign to set up a pilot neighborhood project to produce solar energy. We signed. The United States signed. A great breakthrough, right? No.

Ronald Reagan was elected president in 1980, defeating Jimmy Carter. He ordered the solar collectors removed from the White House. He appointed new officials to the Department of Energy. They told us to forget about the solar energy action project. "But we have a contract with the United States!" we said. "Take it to court," they chortled. "Even if you win, it will take three years. What will you do to buy food and pay the rent in the meantime?"

Why did that happen? For an answer we need to look at the other arena when the truth of planetary danger was known. That was in the offices of Exxon, where research and development staff in the mid '70s began warning that heating Earth by pouring into our air the heat-trapping gases emitted by burning fossil fuels—the core of Exxon's business plan—was, in the long run, extremely dangerous. It became clear that Exxon had two basic choices: with deliberate planful speed, to make a major change in their business plan, or to lie about the danger and convince the public there was nothing to worry about. They chose to lie. To make many people and other life-forms die. The Spirit and its intrinsic love was defeated. The Torah in its best truth was defaced.

Not till 2022, with the passage of the misnamed Inflation Reduction Act, did the United States government get where President Carter had tried to bring it. It took from 1977 to 2022 to pass the first serious law to address the climate crisis. Almost fifty years wasted in just beginning to deal with the most serious crisis in human history. At the same time, from the standpoint of beleaguered climate activists, not quite wasted. Our numbers slowly grew with the numbers suddenly leaping as the disasters we warned about turned real: fires, floods, famines, disease.

For myself, the Carter surge in wisdom was an activation, and the Reagan failure taught me that normal politics was necessary but not enough. I realized "the era of big government is over" really meant "the era of caring for each other is over" and "the era of caring for Earth must not begin."

The failure of concern for planet Earth was a spiritual failure, the defeat of love by greed—and it would take a new great awakening to embody love for Earth into the technologies and politics to save her/ him/ them.

***

In 1998, I turned sixty-five. Phyllis suggested celebrating with a birthday party. I said yes, but only if it were also a spiritually and politically powerful action.

We talked with Rabbi Jeff Roth at Elat Chayyim and agreed on the seventh day of Sukkot, called *Hoshana Rabbah*—"the Great Save Us." Hoshana Rabbah traditionally includes breaking willow branches to mark the end of the Sukkot ritual of waving four species into the Breath of Life. The willows were contributed by Elat Chayyim from its profusion of weeping willow trees.

Save us from what? When we reread the seven "save us" prayers, we realized they were mostly about saving Earth from pollution and poison. So we decided to create an action on the banks of the Hudson River, which had been thoroughly poisoned by General Electric's dumping cancer-causing PCBs into the water. We decided to dedicate the seven prayers to the seven days of Creation. Participants created seven large banners from bedsheets: blue for the oceans, yellow for sun, moon, and stars, white for Shabbat, and so on. For each day, they created a dance with its own melody and color.

Rabbi Shefa Gold wrapped up Sukkot with a profound insight: "People talk about waving the *etrog* (lemony fruit) and *lulav* (palm branch) in the six directions of the world (up, down, left, right, front, back). But there are seven. We are told after each waving to bring them to our heart. The seventh direction is inward. Shabbat in space."

About three hundred people showed up and took delighted part in the rituals and in signing a petition to New York authorities to crack down on GE's poisoning of the river. There were rabbinical students from Manhattan; nuns who lived in convents all along the Hudson; one Iroquois spiritual leader who said he read in the newspaper that we were trying to clean up the river, so he felt he needed to come; and the renowned folk singer Pete Seeger, who led the ship Clearwater in its eco-friendly mission on the Hudson and sang for us in a cracked voice a couple of Hebrew songs. All along we felt the Spirit dancing and singing with us.

* * *

Sometime around 2006, the Church of Sweden through the Archbishop of Uppsala called together a World Interfaith Summit on the Climate Crisis. The inaugural service was typical interfaith: Jews blew shofar, Buddhists rang a bell, Muslims chanted from the Quran, and all the others shone their best light into the world. Then, down the center aisle of the ancient cathedral rolled a six-feet-high green globe, made of green moss.

A gasp from everyone. This was the symbol of no one tradition. It could be—should be—a symbol of all the cultures and traditions. I could hear the Spirit dancing as the great globe rolled.

* * *

The Chautauqua Institution began as a nineteenth-century town for Protestant spiritual exploration. By the 2020s it had become a much more universal retreat center that every summer drew at least ten thousand people to explore their own and each others' values, yearnings, and commitments. In one of those summers, I was invited by Chautauqua's department of religion to speak on "What is Radicalism?"

I came to the speech dressed in a red shirt and white pants. "Why am I dressed like this?" I asked. "Because these are the colors of a radish. And the words radish and radical come from the same root in Latin. The root means 'root.'"

For me, the root was, and is, Torah. Having given the crowd something to chuckle about and think about, I turned to exploring what it meant to see Torah as the radical root of my life and especially my action for justice and for peace. I explained what was new for most of the crowd, that Torah cared passionately for Earth and to protect and heal Earth, invented the whole idea of a sabbatical year in which human beings would let the Earth rest. Justice and peace had to extend beyond the human species if humanity and life were to thrive.

When I finished, one of the audience evidently hoped to catch the rabbi in a contradiction: "What do you do with 'Multiply, fill up the Earth, and subdue it'?"

I said, "Done! Now what?" The audience exploded with applause.

I added, "Traditional Judaism would say that if you put on *t'fillin* (small black boxes filled with words from the Torah attached to arm and forehead in prayer) in the morning, you shouldn't put on t'fillin in the afternoon. Maybe the goal of the Torah we have was to fill the Earth with human beings to the point at which humanity and all the rest of life could live and thrive. We have reached that point and are hovering in the danger of using our total domination to total the planet. A metaphor from what we mean when we say 'Total the car.'"

Then I went one step further. I reminded them I had said, "Now what?" For me, this means a new level of Torah. At its heart must be the Song of Songs. For in the Song beyond all Songs is a celebration of the lovely Earth and lovable, loving human beings. The Song is not utopia. In its verses are one or two incidents of violence. Whereas in most of our lives, violence is endemic, and the loving peace comes only in small moments; in the Song there is a world of loving peace and only a few moments of violence. I think those troubled moments come to tell us that the world of the Song can actually be achieved; it is not a fantasy.

※ ※ ※

I was on vacation at Cape May, New Jersey, just across the bay from Delaware. It was a delicious time with Phyllis and other family, including our ten-month-old granddaughter, who is a hoot.

I was also deeply involved in a work project I found delicious: transforming Tisha B'Av, the ancient day of tears and fasting in memory of two ancient Temples in Jerusalem. They were burned by ancient Empires—Babylonia and Rome. Now, could we get people to lament, hope, and act for our endangered universal Temple, Earth?

My granddaughter is named Yaela. She loved it when I sang or whistled to her. She would bob up and down, dancing to the rhythm. One morning, sitting on the beach, she started a conversation with some seagulls. She babbled, they squawked. She babbled some more, they squawked some more. I began to sing to her that great psalm of our own generation, "Morning Has Broken":

> Morning has broken like the first morning;
> Blackbird has spoken like the first bird.
> Praise for the singing! Praise for the morning!
> Praise for them springing fresh from the Word!

And then my voice broke, tears sprang to my eyes. Here we were, in the summer of the great oil gusher in the Gulf, where petrels and pelicans were dying in the sludge, and I was singing in joy for God's morning and God's blackbird—while Yaela conversed with a seagull. I wondered: what Earth, what oceans, are we bequeathing her? Will her child someday be able to sit beside the great Atlantic as the waves come rolling in, not poisoned by our oil? Will her child someday be able to babble with the seagulls, not dying breathless as the breathing name of God, YHWH, collapses in exhaustion?

That is why I need to do the work, even on vacation. That is why we gather at the Capitol on Tisha B'Av, the day we grieve our imperiled Temple, Earth. The day we turn hope into action to face a Senate that is besmirched with oily money, and therefore will not act to heal Earth from the climate crisis that besets us, and leave to Yaela's child, a generation hence, seagulls she can sing with. The Spirit hums a sad song that befits my tears, then modulates into a marching melody as I try to transform the day of mourning into active hope.

16
Ishmael and Isaac

By 1974, I had learned enough Judaism that it made sense for Fabrangen's Rosh Hashanah steering committee to invite me to lead the prayer service for the first evening of the festival. I asked myself what Rosh Hashanah and the whole month of *Tishrei* were really about, and how to connect our Jewish and our American lives. I decided that Tishrei was really about water—the importance of rain and then of dew to make the herding and the farming fruitful. Then I asked myself, what's the sacred American text about yearning for water?

What came to me was the first chapter of the great novel *Moby-Dick*. It describes the people of Manhattan yearning for the sea, some of them yearning to sail in whaling boats, others simply yearning to visit the edge of the island where ocean stretched out in waves of water. The book begins with a sentence of three words—"Call me Ishmael." So for prayer on Rosh Hashanah evening, I brought that line and several water-yearning paragraphs to freshen the community.

The next morning, the person who had been assigned to give order to the passages of Torah asked me whether I would want to take an *aliyah*, a visit to the central platform where the Torah would be read. Once there, my job would be to say a blessing for the reading. I said yes.

Next question, you would think easier, but in this case a lot harder: "What's your Hebrew name to call you up by?"

I flashed to the night before. I had quoted Herman Melville and turned the first paragraph of *Moby-Dick* into a prayer. So when I'd said "Call me Ishmael," I was speaking to God. Did I mean it? I decided that I did. So I answered him, "*Avraham Yitzhak Yishmael.*" He looked at me, startled. "That's not your name! Where does this Yishmael come from? I'll give you another five minutes. You make sure that you want what you're saying; you can let me know in five minutes."

It wasn't just *Moby-Dick* and whale ships that tumbled through my mind. Was I naming myself Ishmael in part because I felt willing to share a Palestinian identity? And if so, what does that feel like? I felt the Spirit giving me a gentle shove toward a blackboard where "Yishmael" was written. I remembered 1969 when it was still possible for me and other American Jews and maybe anybody to go deep into the Dome of the Rock in Jerusalem. Its beauty was shaped by Muslims in a space that Jews call the Temple Mount, that Muslims call the Noble Sanctuary. I was welcomed not only into the Dome but to walk down a narrow spiral staircase into the heart of the Rock itself. This was where, according to Jewish tradition, Isaac was stretched out and bound, ready to be offered by his father to bring God near. This is where, according to Muslim tradition, the Prophet Mohammad, peace be upon him, leaped off for a mystical voyage to heaven. Would adding Ishmael to my name change my self into a sometimes Muslim? How far was I willing to go with this?

I went far enough to be awe-struck by the Rock. And perhaps it is a meteor that fell to Earth millennia before Isaac or Mohammad trod Earth. The true answer: the future would take me, and I would go as far as it carried me. So when the Rosh Hashanah name-crier appeared again a few minutes later, I was willing. "Yes," I said, "Call me Ishmael. Call me *Avraham Yitzhak, Yishmael.*" He looked at me, shrugged, and called out my new name.

There was a guffaw of laughter from, I saw, as I glanced around, a good friend of mine—Jeff Marker. He was not yet ordained, but he would soon become a Conservative radical rabbi. He was laughing his head off. For an instant I was furious. How dare he laugh at my risky wrestling with a change of name. Then I realized: the whole story in the Bible is full of laughter. Abraham and Sarah laughed when the divine messengers told them that they were going to have a child. Sarah laughed as she said to the angelic being, "I don't have my monthlies anymore, and the old man can't even get it up. What's the joke, we should have a kid?"

But the angel had the last laugh. They had a boy and named him "Laughing-one," in Hebrew, *Yitzhak*; in anglicized Hebrew, Isaac. His older half-brother, Ishmael, loved to laugh along with him. But his semi-foster mother Sarah accused Ishmael of laughing at his younger brother, Laughing-one. She was so distressed that she wanted Ishmael sent out of Abraham's tent. Maybe she felt that his identity was so similar to her son's that Ishmael would be a cloudy mirror to Isaac if they grew up together.

So practically everybody in the story laughed, and Jeff Marker's laughter was like the divine seal that I had made the proper choice. If there had been no laughter in our contemporary story, it would have meant my choice was a mistake. At least that's what I decided. And I could hear the Spirit laughing as the full meaning of the story sank into our lives.

I remembered afterward that on my trip to Israel and Occupied Palestine in 1969, I had visited the mystics' town of *Tz'fat* (Safed). I saw a painting of the Dome of the Rock on the roof of one of the mystical shuls in this town of rich Jewish creativity. I blinked. The Israeli guide, almost audibly sneering at the dumb American visitor, asked, "So why do you think the Dome is on the ceiling?" I said, "Of course it's a marker for the future Third Temple." He looked at me, a little stunned at what I guess he thought was at least one correct answer.

Having stepped into the deepest core of the Dome of the Rock, having seen it in this Jewish mystics' shul in the great mystical town, having named myself for rising to the Torah as partly Ishmael, I decided to get myself a *tallis*, a prayer shawl, with three images woven into it: the Dome of the Rock, the Western Wall, and between them the Rock where Isaac was bound and Mohammad leaped off for heaven. I found the weaver, she wove the tallis. Years later, the cloth started to unravel. Phyllis arranged for the original weaver to do some reweaving and make the tallis new again. Ever since I took the name, "Call me Ishmael," when Israel and stateless Palestine have traded wars with each other, I've felt myself divided, torn. When—rarely—they were peaceful, I could be, as well.

When I told Reb Zalman this long tale, he said I shouldn't be afraid. It would be a *m'chayeh* (life-giving practice) for every Jew to take on the name Ishmael or Hagar and every Muslim, Isaac or Sarah. "Maybe then," he said, "instead of feeling torn by war between us, we could recover the wider tent of Abraham and join our joy to the peoples' peace."

And literally, as I tap letter by letter in the writing of this story, Spirit speaks to me about its hidden meaning. The biblical Ishmael was a water-seeker! Like Melville's all Manhattan. No wonder Melville named his ocean-thirsty hero as he did. The biblical Ishmael was about to die of thirst when his mother Hagar called forth the waters of a well to nourish him. To thank the God who gave them water, she named the well, *"Be'er Lachai Ro'i,* Wellspring of the Living One Who Sees Me." It has taken me and Spirit fifty years to tie together all the meanings of this tale. Blessed be the Infinite, the ONE, who sees us, nurtures us with water and with wisdom.

※ ※ ※

In mid-November 1977, the Israeli English-language magazine *New Outlook* held a peace-oriented conference in Tel Aviv. It had supported a two-state peace with occupied Palestinians and was looking to build more support for the idea. In the middle of the conference, President of Egypt Anwar Sadat announced he would visit Jerusalem on November 19-21. What to do? The conference organizers decided to suspend the conference for two days and return when this astonishing peacemaking event was complete. All the conferees scurried off to be present for peace.

We returned two days later, full of our observations of how Israelis were taking the prospect of peace between Israel and its biggest adversary. "A family I barely knew invited me to dinner," said one conferee. "In the middle of the meal, the mother among our hosts abruptly put down her spoon, saying, 'Every year before the birth of our children, I prayed each one would be a girl so she would not go into the Army and get killed.' She burst into tears. Her husband, astonished, said, 'You never said such a thing to me before!' She answered, 'It never would have mattered before. Now it matters.'"

Sadat came to Camp David to work out the terms of peace, and came out of that august meeting looking as if he had signed his own death warrant. He had. The deal he struck did not include anything for the Palestinians.

An Egyptian passionately committed to Palestine and enraged by the failure to win them anything killed President Sadat. The Spirit fell and kept on falling. It paused for a bit with the Oslo Accords between Israel and the Palestinians but fell precipitously when Israeli Prime Minister Rabin was murdered by a right-wing Israeli for daring to try peace with Palestine. From then until the present moment, for Palestinians and for all Jews committed to justice, the Spirit has fallen and fallen.

* * *

In 1988, Rabbi Brian Walt was the rabbi of a Reconstructionist congregation in the Philadelphia suburbs. He was a young RRC graduate and an immigrant from South Africa. He said he had been an anti-apartheid activist and knew he was risking a life in prison.

Only one person in his large family, Aunt Ethel, took part in a public challenge to apartheid, root and branch. She joined in the weekly "Black Sash" silent vigils of women opposing apartheid. The relationship both challenged him and inspired him. How could he be that brave and not spend his life in prison? Then he read that in America there was a group called "Jews for Urban Justice," and he decided if such a group could exist, he was going to find it. So he came, and he enrolled at RRC.

While he was "rabbinating" in the suburban congregation, one of the recurring wars led by the Israeli government and the Hamas leadership of Palestinians in Gaza was in full flame. He said the Mourner's *Kaddish* for the Israeli dead in that war, and added a totally new phrase. The prayer pleads with God who knew how to create harmony in the ultimate reaches of the universe, to teach us to create harmony within ourselves, and peace for the Jewish people. Some also add "for all who dwell on Earth." But Brian added a very brief reference—"for all the children of Ishmael"—immediately after "for all the children of Israel."

Then, in the midst of the first intifada, Brian led a group of us in the heart of the city, at the Israeli consulate, in a vigil of sorrow about the deaths of Israelis and Palestinians during that struggle. At the end of the vigil, he led us in saying the Mourner's Kaddish for all those people, of both communities. And he told his congregation that he had lit a *yahrzeit* candle for all the dead.

These two actions led to a deep internal debate in his congregation, many of whose members were deeply distressed that he included Palestinians. Brian told them that although his contract had more than a year yet to run, he didn't think he could be an adequate and effective rabbi unless two-thirds of the congregation voted to renew it. They took a vote, and while more than a majority voted to renew his tenure, it wasn't quite two-thirds. Brian felt that it wouldn't work for him to keep on being their spiritual leader.

So then a number of members of the congregation, plus a sizable number of Philadelphians—many of them members of New Jewish Agenda, many of them activists who had never been members of any synagogue before—joined in shaping a new congregation, Mishkan Shalom, with Brian as its rabbi. The shaping included a congregational commitment to support the creation of a new Palestinian state at peace with Israel, to support the full presence and equality of gay and lesbian people in the Jewish world and in the world beyond, and to work on behalf of the poor and disempowered in the city of Philadelphia. At that time there was no other synagogue in America that took on those commitments and that covenant.

These commitments have not only entered our public action in the world but have also entered bits and pieces of our liturgy. When Brian heard about or perhaps directly experienced—I can't remember which—the practice we had adopted at Elat Chayyim of adding *"v'al kol Yishmael"* (and upon all the children of Yishmael) to the Kaddish, he brought it to Mishkan.

He also brought our practice of sometimes using *"Od yavo shalom aleynu"* (may peace come upon us) as the *Aleynu* prayer, not despite but because of its transgressive use of Arabic in a Hebrew prayer "Salaam!" (Peace!), exemplified the same commitment. Mishkan has continued to pioneer on similar issues and on some transformations of liturgy as they have arisen all these years.

What's more, Brian chose to become the executive director of a new organization, Rabbis for Human Rights/North America (now called *T'ruah*) to defend human rights in Israel/Palestine and in the U.S. Mishkan Shalom supported his doing this work at the same time he was a beloved and effective congregational rabbi.

I could hear the Spirit breathing through a shofar song of Liturgy and Liberation.

※ ※ ※

On a spring morning in 1994, I'd just awakened from a pleasant sleep after celebrating the raucous, rowdy, hilarious, spring-fever *Purim* festival the night before. Purim is intertwined with the Scroll of Esther, in which a pompous king and a wicked prime minister are ultimately outwitted by a wise Jewish courtier and a courageous Jewish queen. At one level, the story is about a genocidal threat aimed at the Jews. By echoing an earlier genocidal threat from the tribe of Amalek, the story turns the danger into an archetype. To this threat the Jews respond with diplomatic wisdom and, ultimately, a delicious revenge.

At another level, the story is a joke: What you intend to do to me, that's what happens to you. So, the wicked Haman would hang the Jews? He ends up swinging from his own gallows. So, the pompous king refuses to take orders from a woman? He ends by doing exactly what his Queen tells him to do.

When I say the Scroll of Esther and the Purim festival are intertwined, I am choosing my words with care. In the official version of Jewish history and ritual, the story of Queen Esther led to the celebration of Purim. Today, many scholars think it went the other way: A ribald festival of early spring was justified by a hilarious novella: the Scroll of Esther. All agree that the two are intertwined.

From the easy laughter of a Purim evening—reading the Scroll of Esther with its scathing humor aimed at kings and ministers; rattling my noisemaker at every mention of the name of wicked Haman; joining in the bawdy plays called *Purimspiels* that poked fun at rabbis, Torah, Jews, at God's Own Self for choosing to be absent from this book.

From all this reverly, I woke to hear a news story on the radio. Some religious Jew named *Baruch* ("Blessed") had walked with a machine gun into the Cave of Machpelah in Hebron, the Tomb of Abraham and Sarah, and there had murdered twenty-nine of his cousins, the children of Abraham's other family, who were praying prostrate on their faces. From behind. At prayer. For the sake of God.

Yes, for God he killed them, for the God to whom they were at the very same moment praying. Killed them because it was Purim, the moment when we are to remember to blot out the name of Amalek, the archetypal murderer who had assailed us from the rear, killed us when we were helpless. He turned his machine gun into a midrash.

The Talmud says that on Purim we are to get just drunk enough to not know the difference between "Blessed Mordechai" and "Cursed Haman." Between Baruch/Blessed, and Aror/Cursed. For Purim is the day of inversions, inside-outs, of turning the world upside-down. Hilarity and grotesquerie.

This man had become so drunk on blood that he could no longer tell the difference in his own identity between Baruch/Blessed, and Aror/Cursed; between becoming the murderer Haman and becoming the healer Mordechai. And I could not help repeating and repeating, I who had written so many creative *midrashim* on a typewriter, he had written a deadly midrash with his gun. I lay in bed, drowning out this new name of Amalek as it came pouring from the radio, saying, shouting, screaming, wailing, "No no no no no no no."

Twenty-five years of joyful prayer and midrash, shattered with one gun and twenty-nine lives. Twenty-five years of hope and anger, grief and loneliness, rolling the spiral of the Scroll, walking the spiral of the festivals, learning the Hebrew puns that point the path to Torah meaning. No no no no no no no. The Black Hole of Torah, sucking in all light, all meaning.

At last I got out of bed. I called my children, my friends, my teachers, my students. We began to weave a counter-midrash, a weave of tears and healing, not of blood and bullets. For it to have power may take years, decades, centuries in which it grows from seed to sprout to Tree of Life. From this abysmal fall of Spirit, we worked to make a life-giving understanding of the whole Amalek mythos. Would it work? We did not know.

In moments of darkness—not from them, but within them—I glimpse new Torah: a Torah in which the Jewish people are empowered in the world and so can create, must create, new Torah for a people no longer slaves and outcasts. And an "aiming" for all peoples struggling for freedom. Torah for a people who must not claim freedom while becoming slave-masters and pharaohs. In Hebrew, *ruach* means "breath, wind, spirit," all at once. That is especially apt in this moment of our yearning, our action, and our prayer: Holy Spirit, Breath of all life, we need Your help. Become a Wind of Change!

* * *

In 2002, Phyllis and I were in Jerusalem, invited to speak as outside observers to a group headed by a (Jewish) Zen Buddhist leader, Bernie Glassman. While we were there, Rabbi Arik Ascherman invited us to visit the Palestinian village of Hares near Jerusalem. We did, and he showed us the pillaged olive trees of the village, destroyed by Israeli settlers and the IDF. We were shocked, shaken. But I blurted, "I know what to do about that!"

I was referring to a "Trees for Vietnam" campaign thirty years earlier, as a Jewish response to U.S. efforts with Agent Orange to destroy Vietnamese forests—"Jewish" in the light of Deuteronomy's prohibition on destroying even or especially "enemy" trees.

Back in the States, together with Rabbi Mordechai Liebling and Cherie Brown (director of the National Coalition-Building Institute and leader of a large Jewish subgroup of reevaluation counselors), we started an "Olive Trees for Peace" campaign. It raised more than $200,000 to support Rabbis for Human Rights in Israel. One of our most successful efforts was an ad in *The New York Times*. Mordechai recalls it cost $50,000. We put in a coupon inviting contributions and by far repaid the cost, with a lot of money left over for RHR. The success of "Olive Trees for Peace" convinced Rabbi Brian Walt and others that a North American Rabbis for Human Rights could support itself and help support RHR in Israel as well. Our effort became a "proof of concept," and we became the founders of what is now T'ruah.

I am telling the whole story because it exemplifies what can be done when emotions are high and activists are—well, active. Success takes a roused and rising Spirit, too. That depends on whether there is a super-saturated solution of people ready to breathe together and open themselves to a seed-like crystal. If there is, the response is far more likely to be a rush of change, as a whole super-saturated solution becomes a sparkling crystal. There was.

※ ※ ※

In the midst of a very busy day shortly before Thanksgiving in 2006, my phone rang. It was Imam Mahdi Bray of the Muslim American Society Freedom Foundation, whom I had met in several vigils against the use of torture by the U.S. government. He called to tell me the following story and to ask for help.

A few days earlier, six imams on their way home from a conference of imams were forced off a US Airways flight in handcuffs because they'd been praying before entering the plane. Although they had gone through security and in every other way satisfied security requirements, someone on the plane wrote a note to an attendant: their presence made him or her uncomfortable. So the airline attendants forced the imams off the plane in handcuffs, and even after checking on their *bona fides* refused to let them board another flight.

So Imam Mahdi asked me: would I join a pray-in by Jews, Christians, and Muslims at Washington National Airport on the next Monday morning?

I groaned. I'd intended to come back home to Philadelphia on Sunday evening from a family Thanksgiving visit to the Midwest. To get to Washington in time, I would have to switch my flight and stay overnight in Washington. I thought, *I'm sorry, really sorry—but I really can't do it*. But then there surfaced in my head a long buried memory.

My grandmother was born in Poland and came to America in 1906 in her teens. When I was about eleven, in 1944, she came home in tears from a visit to the kosher butcher in our neighborhood. I asked her what was wrong, and she explained: two of the women in the buying line had used a derogatory Yiddish word about African-Americans, and my grandmother had spoken up: "You must not talk that way! In Europe, that is the way they talked about us! This is America, and you must not talk that way!"

So when I actually spoke on the telephone to Imam Bray, what came out of my mouth was, "Yes, of course." And at the pray-in I told the story and then I added: "That is why I am here today. My community knows very well that what might seem small acts of contempt, of dehumanization, can grow into mountains of death and disaster. So I am here to say to US Air: "This is America! You must not act this way!"

After leaders of each community spoke, the Muslims prayed in the traditional way, through prostration and chant. Then I chanted the traditional prayer for peace with a significant addition: *Oseh shalom bimromav, hu yaaseh shalom aleynu, v'al kol Yisrael—v'al kol Yishmael—v'al kol yoshvei tevel.* "You Who make shalom, harmony, peace, in the ultimate reaches of the universe, teach us to make shalom, peace, within us, among us; for all the Godwrestling folk, the people Yisrael; for all our cousins the children of Ishmael; and among all who dwell upon this planet."

Several Christian ministers drew on the prayers of their own tradition for justice, for peace, for prayer itself. And to all these prayers we together said: *Ameyn, ahmin*, amen.

***

In 2016, Israel invaded Lebanon for the second time. As usual, there were growing numbers of deaths of soldiers and civilians on both sides. So I found myself wanting to write an English translation of the Mourner's Kaddish.

There was a lot I wanted to unfold from the traditional Aramaic and Hebrew text, but the sharpest point for me was one strange word. The Aramaic celebrates God by saying that there are many songs, praises, offerings, that we would want to bring to the God that is the Breath of Life but that we cannot bring enough to match the real glory of the Infinite One. Among the words of what we would like to bring but cannot is the word "*Nechamata*, consolation." That is not a word of celebration or glorification. Why would we want to bring consolation, and why can't we bring enough—or any at all?

It seemed to me that there are many kinds of deaths in a world, and for most of them God welcomes words of consolation. Indeed, death seems to be an essential part of the flow of life, an aspect of God's world that is part of the great design. But when some human beings made in the image of God deliberately kill others made in the image of God, there is no way to console God for those deaths.

As I jotted down a sentence of translation to make clear why that word is in the midst of a text where the rest of the praise of the Breath of Life is so different, I could feel the Spirit trying to console me. I had no illusions about the Spirit's fall in this time of killing. Yet I could hear the Spirit muttering that simply pointing out the impossibility of consoling God for murder or for war would itself be a service to the Breath of Life.

17
Bashert

The summer of 1982 was a magical encounter with the Spirit. Phyllis and I were each in the midst of an adventure in love. Not with each other, but each of us with someone other.

For me there was the excitement of preparing to teach rabbis that fall at RRC, the excitement of moving to Philadelphia, the agonizing excitement of the Israeli war against parts of Lebanon. Even listening to the radio changed for me in profound ways. Living in Washington, I had never bothered to listen to National Public Radio because the daily political life of the city was "NPR" all around me 24/7. But in Philadelphia, I missed that vibe and began listening to WHYY every morning.

Phyllis was on the board of B'nai Or and came to Philadelphia fairly often to take part in board meetings. I was living in a rented house because I didn't know whether I was going to stay in Philadelphia. It had plenty of room for visitors, so Phyllis and sometimes her two children would stay in that house when she came to Philadelphia.

I think once two people, as we had at the Havurah Institute of 1982, talked about love,* there's always likely to be a different aura to their friendship. But with each of us in a different loving relationship, the aura was almost hidden. Until one day, shortly after Phyllis turned forty years old, said to me, "If we are going to continue being

---

* As described in the Afterword by Phyllis Ocean Berman.

friends, I think you'll need to know what I really look like." And she took off the wig that I soon discovered she'd been wearing for twenty years since her hair decided it was allergic to her, or maybe vice-versa, and fell out. I looked at her with her head bald and glowing and said, in a burst of feeling that had very little thought behind it, "You are the most beautiful martian in the world!"

She explained the whole history of her disappeared hair and her wig camouflage. Her parents had suggested that she get a series of expensive wigs, especially expensive for a family that planned carefully each dollar, and she agreed. But there were several incidents that began to convince her that the wig was more a snare than a shield. One was that she went dancing with a rabbinical student at Jewish Theological Seminary (JTS), some months after graduating from college, for the evening of *Simchat Torah*. In the wonderfully wild dance, she fell and her wig fell off. Her escort at the dance did not know how to ease an embarrassing moment. The result was that for decades, Phyllis would not enter the halls of JTS. It was trauma territory.

As her fortieth birthday approached, Phyllis began to wonder if she could dare to get rid of the wig and appear as she really was. She created a birthday party during Hanukkah of 1982 and gathered her closest friends for a ritual of bringing more light and openness into the world—and took off her wig. She was greeted not with upset or fear but with joy and welcome. She was still in that mood when next she came to Philadelphia and took off her wig for me.

Thank God, she took the "beautiful martian" exclamation as indeed the warm and excited compliment I meant it to be. Meanwhile, each of our relationships broke up. Phyllis and I turned toward each other.

Then my previous relationship sputtered alight for a moment, and Phyllis told me not to stay in touch with her until I had made up my mind. It took only a few weeks for me to be clear that the old relationship was over. Phyllis and I reconnected.

"*Bashert*," they say, is the word for fate intervening through heightened love. That's what happened.

*　＊　＊*

We decided to get married on a day that was both the summer solstice and a full moon. (We had chosen a different day, but all our children said they had final exams that week.) We made a symbolic big deal out of affirming "the fullness of the sun and the fullness of the moon"—connecting that with our commitment to the equality of women (the moon) and men (the sun).

We also added "Ocean" as a middle name to both our names, and under the *chuppah* we poured together water from the Atlantic, the Pacific, and the Mediterranean to symbolize our unity as Ocean.

We had asked Rabbi Max Ticktin and Esther Ticktin, precious old friends of us both long before we knew each other, to be the rabbinic guardians and officiants for our wedding ceremony. Under the chuppah, Esther looked us both in the eyes and said: "Just remember: it is not the sun and moon who are getting married here. It is not the Atlantic and Pacific who are getting married here. It is Phyllis and Arthur who are getting married here. Don't forget!"

Our wedding guests cheered!

Within, beneath, and beyond all the treasury of Jewish symbol and story, the truth: Don't forget how down-to-earth it needs to be.

*　＊　＊*

Once while Phyllis and I were in Jamaica, she began to notice that she was attracting some unpleasant public attention. She'd stopped wearing a wig or turban to hide her bald head long ago. Seeing her now, a number of people were making a hand symbol "against the evil eye." In a most joyful stay, it was an upsetting intrusion.

I suggested that maybe some Rastafarians, who had strongly affirmed and encouraged wearing hair in dreadlocks, were seeing baldness as a religious threat. Our friend Rabbi Jack Gabriel had given us contact information for a Rastafarian elder whom he admired. So we called and arranged to meet him. For about an hour, we had a pleasant conversation. Then I explained the problem Phyllis had been facing and asked, could Rastafarian beliefs have led to this aversion toward her baldness? He drew himself up and said with simple dignity, "To a true Rastafarian, the hair is on the inside!" The universal Spirit smiled invisibly. We were honored to have met a "true Rastafarian," and took more joy in our travels.

※ ※ ※

Phyllis is my favorite rabbi. She spent more than thirty years imagining, inventing, and bringing to full reality a school for immigrants from all over the world to learn how to speak and understand English so they would be able to function in North America with jobs and education and so on. One of the most important aspects of Phyllis' life was a silent meditation retreat led by Rabbi David Cooper and Shoshana Cooper, every six months a full week of silence and meditation. Phyllis reported that these meditation retreats were crucial to her work and her sanity. She said it would take each time about three days to settle into the silence and begin to feel the fullness of her own reality. One week, she came back home reporting she had actually seen and heard the *crack* of dawn. She explained that it took long silence to make that possible.

For most of those occasions, I was left alone at home. I could make my way for a week on my own. So as not to interrupt Phyllis' silence, I would not call her except in a real emergency.

During one of those retreats, on the second or third day I found myself in what felt like a real crisis. I could not find the keys to the house and the car. Without them, I would be imprisoned in our house. I searched frantically. Every room. Never had I been so earnest in my search for anything, and never was I so distraught at failing to find those keys. In despair, I did what we had agreed I would only do in a real emergency—I called Phyllis at the silent retreat to ask her to speak if she had any idea where the keys might be.

She had me walk through the entire house and place after place that seemed a reasonable possibility. Nothing at all. The last room to be explored was our bedroom. Patiently, Phyllis had me walk around the room. A wastebasket here, a desk drawer there. Nothing at all. Then she said, "Walk over to the bed." I did. "Turn back the covers on my side of the bed." I did. There were the keys. I said, "You are the key to my life."

18

Illness, Death, and Grief

In 2009, I was part of what could have been a horrendous car crash, but was horrendous only for the car. I was picking up my grandson Elior at a rest stop halfway to Washington, DC. His father had driven him the first half of the journey, and I was doing the second half so he could spend time with Phyllis and me. The edges of a huge hurricane came down in sheets of water and forced me to slow down a great deal. Behind me a car was not so quick to get the message and bumped me hard from behind. My car careened into a center fence on the highway, crashing to a halt. Elior was in the back seat. I took a deep breath, turned my head, and said, "Elior, how are you?" He waited about five seconds of self-evaluation to answer: "I'm okay."

I thought that I was also okay, and then I wanted to get out of the car. But I was swarmed by other motorists who had stopped in the hurricane downpour and were yelling that I must wait for the police and for an ambulance. As I did so, it became clear that something was wrong with my knee.

The crash had broken one bone in the knee and it needed an operation with the substitution of a titanium plate to make it work right. The operation itself, though necessary, did more damage to my body. General anesthesia had the effect of putting my bladder, along with the rest of me, to sleep. The bladder did not wake up. For three months I suffered intense pain when a catheter was inserted or removed through my penis. Doctors laughed off my pain as the result of male anxiety. Until my fourth urologist, the good one, said, "No! For most men, the prostate gland sits parallel to the bladder. In ten percent of men, it is perpendicular, and insertion of the catheter can cause intense pain. But there is a solution—a suprapubic catheter inserted directly through a small incision into the bladder itself." He did the simple surgery. It worked, and met my needs with no pain. In about six weeks, the bladder had awakened.

* * *

It took months of rehabilitation from the car crash for me to walk normally again. The High Holy Days came and went and I was still in rehab by Sukkot.

I loved the fragile, open-airy home that is the *sukkah* Jews traditionally live in for the week of harvest festival. And I love the ritual of shaking three branches and a lemony fruit in the wind as part of the celebration. But there was no sukkah in the rehab center and no branches to wave. So Phyllis and I went exploring everywhere in the facility and came to a tiny open place with no roof and just enough space to put a leafy branch above our heads. And then we wondered about our next-room neighbors who were also Jewish and far more observant than we.

We had heard them talking sadly about how impossible it was to fulfill the commandments of the festival. Hesitantly, we showed them the strange tiny sukkah. We thought they might reject it as too unlike a real sukkah. Instead, they celebrated. "A miracle, a miracle!" the family said. The Spirit found a way to sneak in and celebrate beyond the rules.

* * *

As I came home after appendix/gall bladder surgery, my throat was sore. And sore. One month later, my primary doc said, "Of course! You were intubated for four hours, of course your throat is sore!" But another month later, it was still sore. My doctor hmmed and said,

"They teach us in med school that if you hear hoof beats, figure it's a horse, not a zebra. But every once in a while, it might be a zebra. I think we better have a biopsy." And that was how I learned I had early-stage throat cancer. The intubation that irritated my throat actually was a gift because it helped signal the cancer long before I might otherwise have noticed it.

The treatment was six weeks of radiation, five times a week, and once a week of chemo.

The docs warned me that radiation was necessary, and would be aimed with near pinpoint accuracy, but might hurt my mouth. Maybe I should get a stomach tube, just in case. I laughed. My spouse was a fine cook; my mouth could surely taste her food. They shrugged, "If you change your mind, just let us know! "

So the treatments started. They strapped me in till my head felt utterly immobilized, and then jolted my molecules over and over. One day, as Philadelphia underwent a very rare earthquake, I was frightened the medical staff would run away and leave me tethered and helpless. Of course they didn't. I told my daughter, who is an M.D., about my fear, and she said quietly, "We don't do that."

As the radiation took hold, I lost the ability first to taste, then to swallow, and finally to speak. Not eating, I lost a lot of weight. Phyllis kept telling me that if I didn't eat or drink I would die. But meals were excruciating.

By then, the High Holy Days were again upon us. We went to synagogue for Rosh Hashanah and I could only be there for about an hour because I felt so weak. And we read, as we do every year, the verses: "Who shall live, and who shall die? Who by hunger, who by thirst?"

So when we got home, I began to think: those verses, for years I've thought they were just liturgy, repeated as a formula. Not now. They're all too true. Who shall live, who shall die? Me. It would be easy to die; me by hunger, me by thirst. I just have to keep on not eating, not drinking. To live would be much harder. But there is so much

I love!—Phyllis, Torah, our kids and grandkids! Who shall love, who shall die? So I decided to do hard work to keep on living.

I couldn't speak, so on the computer I wrote Phyllis a love letter. I think it's the only one I ever wrote her—saying what I'd been thinking, and that since I wanted to live and keep on loving her, I would have to get a feeding tube after all. Phyllis, with relief and also nervously, agreed: maybe that would give my burning mouth a chance to heal, and give me some nourishment to help the healing. But she would need to learn this way of feeding.

We went to the hospital the day before the day whose evening begins Yom Kippur with the solemn affirmations of *Kol Nidre*. The surgeon placed a feeding tube into my stomach. The next morning, a nurse showed Phyllis how to use the equipment, and sent us home to wait for a medical supply company to deliver the equipment to our house. When the equipment arrived, it looked nothing like what the hospital had shown us. Phyllis was unable to feed me before we left the house. I had had no feeding since 10 o'clock in the morning.

That Kol Nidre, dear friends of ours were gathering together in one of their homes. There were twelve of us there—ten we knew very well and two, whom we didn't know, were students of Rabbi Jeff Roth. At some point that evening, Jeff asked us all to share where and how we were as we entered Yom Kippur. Seeing me shivering from cold that comes from hunger, my dear Phyllis began to cry. "What's wrong?" the others asked. So Phyllis explained that the feeding tube equipment had arrived, but she didn't know to use it.

One of the two strangers introduced herself. She was a nurse, she said, and would come with us after the service to show Phyllis how to use the equipment. Her name was *Emunah*: from Hebrew, meaning Faith.

So Emunah came home with us and showed Phyllis and one of our closest friends how to use the feeding tube. The next morning and again at lunchtime, Phyllis took me home and gave me a feeding. After the Yom Kippur break the fast, Emunah again came to our home to see how Phyllis was doing and to fine-tune her technique so that she could be sure she was not harming me in any way.

The next day, in our local food co-op, Cheryl, the wife of one of the rabbis in our community, asked Phyllis how the holidays had been, and once again Phyllis began to cry. Since she was working full-time commuting into New York City and her usual schedule kept her away from home at least twelve hours a day. She could feed me for an hour at 5-6 in the morning before showering, dressing, eating, and running to catch the train at 6:45; and she could feed me for an hour when returning home around 6:45 pm most evenings. But that was all.

Cheryl, who is a doctor, told Phyllis that she'd be happy to come over one day a week at lunchtime to feed me, and she'd put a request on the listserv of the congregation to ask for other volunteers. So Phyllis went home and put the same request on the listservs of the two other congregations in our neighborhood with which we were connected. Within an hour, she had many more volunteers than were needed to cover the five week-day lunches. Many of the volunteers were strangers to us.

She deliberately chose people who lived within walking distance of our house so that nothing—like a snowstorm—would prevent them from showing up each midday during the week to feed me. She also chose five others as substitutes. They followed the medical-school model: watch one, do one, teach one—training each of the people in our volunteer community to use the feeding tube equipment correctly and safely. Phyllis insisted that I disengage from the computer where I do most of my work in order to engage with the people who were feeding me. "You should learn about them, listen to them, study Torah with them," she said.

Four weeks later, my mouth began to heal, and I started to eat real food through my real mouth. I was joyful reporting that the first taste to come fully back was dark chocolate. My surgeon came to the house and removed the feeding tube.

It was close to Thanksgiving, and we invited all the volunteers who had helped to keep me alive to come to the prayer service called Havdalah that ends Shabbat on Saturday nights. We fed them—what you sow, that's what you reap!—and told them how deeply grateful we were that, through their help, we had been able to survive and thrive. As the liturgy says—not just a formula, a mechanical repetition: To all of you and all whom you love may each year be a *Shana* (year/ change/ transformation) that is *Tova* (good) and *Metuka* (sweet). May we all be inscribed for another year of life to live in awareness, gratefulness, compassion, and connection.

* * *

There are two stories about the Spirit and my own body that are intertwined. The first one occurred when I was eight years old; the second when I was ninety.

When I was eight and about to start the third grade in an elementary school six blocks from my home in Baltimore, I was diagnosed with rheumatic fever. In that day, there were no medicines to deal with rheumatic fever. The disease could weaken the heart and if the weakening got too strong, many people, including children, died of it. The only response that the doctors knew was going to bed and not exerting oneself at all for a year. That is what they prescribed for me.

My mother took over the job of caring for me. Her first name was Hannah, but hardly anybody called her that. Her family, including my brother and me, and just about everyone we knew, called her "Honey."

So for a year, Honey took care of me. She met my every need. She got lists of books from my third-grade teacher and got the books from the library. She also got lots of other books from the library that she thought would interest me. She washed me. Arranged minimally active ways of getting me to the bathroom. She fed me, she talked with me; there was barely anything I didn't have during that year.

When the year ended, the doctors said my heart was as strong as it should have been, and I could go back to school. So I did. And it turned out that I had learned so much that Ms. Rivkin decided I should skip a piece of the fourth grade—something which was legal on the books of my school but seemed never to have been used. I was assigned to low-exertion sports, like hopscotch and the other kids were told not to push me around because, I was told, I could die.

Now let me turn forward eighty-two years to when I turned ninety in 2023. It was as if the *Ribbono Shel Olam*—the Teacher of the World—woke up and said, "Oy, I haven't been checking on him for a while. Now he is in his nineties. Time for him to start having some trouble breathing. Time for one eye to get very weak. Time for this thing the doctors call essential tremor. All these and a few other afflictions came bouncing down the road almost as soon as I turned ninety.

So for all sorts of intimate aspects of my life, I needed a caretaker. In fact, several kinds of caretakers. My tremor made it hard for me to type without making two or three typographical errors in every sentence. One of these caretakers was Molly Paul who transcribed my talking—like right now, these very words. But the chief caretaker 24/7 was Phyllis, who had her own working life as a spiritual director. Every need I had for unusual care meant that she had to shift how she met with the people she was giving spiritual care. It wasn't easy. Sometimes, with and despite all the love between us, it exploded.

One problem was I was having trouble sleeping. I went to sleep easily the minute I laid down, but then I'd wake up at 3 or 4 am, and if I stirred or got up, or went to work at the computer, that would disturb Phyllis. So I would lie quietly awake, unwilling to steal her uninterrupted sleep for my busy-ness. It did give me time to think about my teaching, as long as I could live with not writing anything down. But my handwriting was such a mess because of the tremor, that that probably wasn't such a loss.

One night in that first year of my falling apart physically, I started imagining what The Shalom Center might do about the oncoming Passover in the midst of terrible bloodshed—more than 30,000 deaths—carried out by an ultra-right-wing government of Israel on tens of thousands of non-combatant Palestinians in Gaza, sparked by an atrocious attack by the regime that governed Gaza against Israeli civilians. We at The Shalom Center had just arranged for people to write and distribute an alternative version of the sacred text for the festival of Purim. But as I lay there thinking about Passover coming in a month, I realized that any version of a Passover Haggadah that suggested the Israeli government was Pharoah in this bloodbath of the day, we would need a lot more rage from many Jews than *The Freedom Seder* had met fifty-five years before, and that was plenty!

Just as I was thinking about that prospect, I found myself—my old body—a quarter inch from falling off the bed. I scrambled myself away from the edge as thoughts of falling off, breaking a hip, and probably dying, burst in my mind. It took me until the next morning to realize that my body and my mind were dancing in sync: my body in a place of comfort even when I couldn't sleep, was just a quarter inch from probable disaster. And my mind imaging how to challenge a government made up of Jews who had forgotten what it meant to be seriously Jewish: who had forgotten justice, compassion, even the biblical rules of near equality with non-Israelites who were living in the land. It was the first time I could remember my body and my mind acting in sync.

As I thought about what this would mean for my caretaker Phyllis, how much more strain this would put upon the two of us, there came to me a single sentence; "Phyllis is not Honey and I am not eight years old." That rang like a mantra in my head, my heart, and my bones.

* * *

I have just barely mentioned that while the world's and the Jewish people's bodies politic were getting more violent and destructive, my own body was beginning to make trouble for the "me" I thought I was.

One eye was consumed with "wet" macular degeneration. My eyes got so complicated that I had to use three different pairs of spectacles: one for distance, one for close reading, and one for the computer. And even with those aids, I needed extra-large type to read.

My teeth multiplied their cavities and a different doctor warned me that the bacteria bred that way could be dangerous to the rest of the body.

My throat had been affected by radiation to deal with a throat cancer. Then, it turned out that twelve years later the radiation affected the muscles for swallowing. A combination of the long-term results of radiation and what the doctors called "an essential tremor" brought not only my fingers but also my voice box to trembling. My voice got weaker, rougher, scratchy.

I started having trouble with breathing. It first broke through in Denver, the Mile-High City where oxygen is thinner than in sea-level Philadelphia. But it turned out that even back home, breathing could be a problem. As a result, I needed a Transcatheter aortic valve replacement, or TAVR, patch to one of the valves of my heart. Several months later, perhaps as a result of the twilight anesthetic to calm my body for the TAVR operation, my bladder decided once again to rest, as it had after the car crash. It didn't wake up, so that I needed a supra-pubic catheter again, this time permanently.

The docs discovered that a troublesome supply of fluid had built up around my lungs and was making it hard for them to expand and contract. My metaphor of God as the Breath of Life turned all to be a medical reality.

My guts got so irregular that I needed a special potion to stave off diarrhea. It didn't always work.

Then, on Yom Kippur afternoon in 2023, hurrying to get to prayer in synagogue, I slipped on a rainy patch of grass and broke an ankle. It took twelve weeks for a doctor with a sense of humor to look at my X-ray and then at me and say, "It is not healing. It is not healing. *It is healed!*" In the meantime, of course, I lost a good bit of mobility and some of my muscles decompensated—which means they got a good bit weaker.

As near as I could tell, my brain worked almost as well as before. A little slower, but I could get to the same creative place. All this was happening or accelerating just after I turned ninety.

I imagined the *Ribbono Shel Olam* caught glimpses of my nonagenarian birthday celebration and said, "Oy, I haven't been paying attention to Waskow's body. There must be some of those 248 sinews that should have been getting clunky, and I didn't pay enough attention. So I will encourage them all to go their natural way—all of them at once." That's certainly how it felt.

And there were two other crises that affected me at the same time. One was that Israel was attacked in an atrocious way by the military wing of Hamas, and the other was that Israel has taken revenge in months-long atrocious attacks of its own against Gaza. The Shalom Center would once have quickly turned to trying to use the crisis to move toward a serious peace negotiation—as thousands of American Jews did. But another turning point came into play—this one internal.

The Shalom Center, which I had led for forty years, would have been hard enough to guide effectively in this crisis if my body had been thirty, or fifty, or seventy, even eighty years old. But at the simplest level, the time I needed to set aside just for doctors' visits made it much harder to spend time listening to all the silent voices that shouted in the scream of bloodshed. I realized that if the Center were to survive me, there needed to be a conscious plan to make that happen. So we created one, with dates and functions and titles and even a real live person.

The person would not be a clone of me. We knew that with having someone replace me, there would be bumps and quivers on the road. It was hard to keep remembering: the fact is, he isn't me; that's a good thing, not a bad thing. In all this turmoil, just accept the reality that there will be bumps and quivers.

The Spirit was on our side in seeking peace through justice. In the ultimate history of Earth and Universe, the slow disintegration of my body was probably good, even an invitation to a deeper consciousness. But still, the awkward business of dying is certainly no pleasure for the protagonist. And Russia's war against Ukraine, Israel's massacres of Gaza, the Chinese repression of Tibetan Buddhists and Muslim Uighurs, seemed evidence of human depravity with no long-term benefit. On balance, Spirit seemed to be falling off a precipice without a landing-place.

And then there were the troubles in my body, putting strain on the most loving relationship in my life. Phyllis had shaped a wonderful second career as a spiritual director, bringing open-hearted ears to listen to the lives of other spiritual seekers and encourage them to deeper insight into themselves, into their inner voice. But suddenly my body and my work needed more care than had been the case for the nearly forty years of our marriage. That meant more of Phyllis' time for me, lots of pressure on her time for her spiritual companions, other family, and intimate friends. It was easy to fall into frustration and anger and exhaustion, which was absolutely not what we wanted.

We needed time to invest in rethinking our responses to each other. How could my body, the source of most of the problem, absorb the truth of the trap and come somewhere new? Struggling together in this new reality, working together on this book as writer and editor, seems to have brought us more intimacy as we dance together, though awkwardly, in an even deeper love than we had experienced in our earlier, more independent lives.

I recently asked one of my docs what estimate he could give me of how long a life I could expect after ninety. He laughed. "You have entered the land of magic, not science. We have no numbers for you." I realized he was right: my question was ridiculous. There is a Yiddish saying: "*Man tracht; Gott lacht.* / Humans scheme; God scoffs."

※ ※ ※

This is a tale that keeps happening. My friends keep dying, most of them younger than I am now. Each one has a companion of the Spirit who reminds me what the Spirit did by joining us: to laugh and to cry out, to share these tales and keep others secret.

Most recently, the death of Rabbi Michael Lerner, for forty years my friend and comrade in the struggle for worldwide justice and compassion. Nine years younger, yet afflicted unto death perhaps by the same sense as mine of the Spirit's utter absence this past year. I had long lovingly depended on him to choose to risk walking closer to the precipice than I would. What would it mean to work for change without him?

Marc Raskin, my close companion, neighbor, teacher, student, co-author, co-activist from 1959 to 1977, and then after a gap of estrangement, a renewed friendship till his death in 2017. Six months younger than I.

My brother Howard, three years younger and far healthier than me all our lives, who became for me the guide in personal life that he wished I had been as older brother.

Each with a full stop after the name, to remind us each was a self, unique. And connected.

Adina Abramowitz. Ellen Bernstein. Rabbi David Cooper. Paul Cowan. Rabbi Rachel Cowan. Reverend Bob Edgar. Todd Gitlin. Rabbi Bruce Goldman. Vincent Harding. Tom Hayden. Rabbi Abraham Joshua Heschel. Warren Hinckle. Rabbi Aryeh Hirschfield. Rabbi Shaya Isenberg. Rabbi Burt Jacobson. Bob Kastenmeier. Hazzan Jack Kessler. Diane Levenberg. Paul Lichterman. Carol Cohen McEldowney. Paul Mendes-Flohr. Ira Silverman. Richard Taylor. Rabbi Harold White. Rabbi David Wolfe-Blank. Almost all died younger than I am now.

And a few who died older than I am now: Rabbi Zalman Schachter-Shalomi. Esther Ticktin. Rabbi Max Ticktin.

May each and all their memories be a blessing and a teaching for me and all who remember them.

19

The Ultimate Crisis in Jewish Values

This is the hardest of all the tales to tell. I have been helped as I prepare to tell it by an unconventional reading of the ancient Israelites' trek in the wilderness. Torah teaches that during the great wilderness journey, God's sometimes absence is a kind of presence, a cloud in which it is impossible to see. To see anything but the cloud itself.

The cloud comes at uncertain times into the *Mishkan*, the shrine of appointment between God and people. The cloud may stay for several weeks or months, during which the people don't move anywhere because they don't know where to move. That's the unknowing part of cloud.

Then the cloud moves, taking the form of fire in which it is possible to see where to go. The fire leads the people to their next stopping place. Perhaps that fire has been kindled from the burning bush itself. Perhaps, like the bush when it first appeared to Moses, it calls forth the people to act on a mission of love and liberation.

But for months we have had only a cloud of dark and death. No fire calling forth love and liberation.

So I've been experiencing the last months of disastrous war and massacre among Israelis and Palestinians as this cloud of unknowing. A time, a space, where I did not know where to move, how to act as the fire of the burning bush would once have shown me. For months, what I am used to as my own creative impulse, knowing what would be most just and compassionate action to take next, has shriveled up. I found myself almost untongued. At an annual venue for my best and strongest thoughts about "What is freedom for me now?"—the Freedom Seder revisited at the National Museum of American Jewish History in Philadelphia—I found myself able to say only *"Two peoples safe and free / From the River to the Sea."*

Not a word of my true feelings: that the present government of the State of Israel threw in the garbage pail every principle of justice and compassion that ancient Torah and modern Jewish philosophers had taught the world. That the Netanyahu government was made up of Jews but could not be called Jewish. Just as the governing of the military wing of Hamas could not be called Muslim. Both warped by fear, greed, rage, trauma.

I took some action—sharing information on gatherings for peace, signing demands for a multilateral ceasefire. But I knew that the Israeli public was too traumatized to pay attention, and the Israeli government was too greedy for more land and more power for them to care about Palestinian suffering. The months from October 7, 2023, to the present (as I review these pages for the last time, in June 2025) have felt not like the falling of the Spirit, but like the Spirit's abandonment of us.

It has been a deep unmooring of my self. A loss of the identity, the consciousness, the past/present/future that has lit the way for me since I started writing *The Freedom Seder* in the fall of 1968.

※ ※ ※

But I am also beginning to feel as if the Spirit is groping to recover from their own trauma. The cloud of unknowing has hesitantly begun to lift. It has begun to renew the active fire of the burning bush. It has begun to show us where next to move. My own creativity in this crisis has begun to percolate.

What has happened to give me this fragile sense of renewed and fragile possibility? I feel a flicker, calling us to move toward a prophetic diaspora rather than stay stuck in rage, trauma, fear, and ultra-violence.

Each of the previous tales in this book is based on a single encounter. This one took me five distinct encounters in late 2024 to begin recovering from a sense of catastrophic utter disappearance of the Spirit. It took these five moments to inspire me that the Spirit was breathing again, recovering from their own trauma.

The first came in reading a new book, *The Necessity of Exile*, by Rabbi Shaul Magid of Dartmouth University—now Harvard. Magid argues that the State-centered version of Zionism has fulfilled its purpose of providing a refuge for endangered Jews and a platform for Jewish culture. And with its purpose fulfilled, the State has puffed up its balloon until the balloon exploded into brutally repressing Palestinians in the West Bank, East Jerusalem, and Gaza.

Magid does not stop there. He explores two old Jewish concepts, "Exile" and "Diaspora," going beyond their geographical meanings of separation from the anciently beloved Land of Israel to their spiritual implications in relation to Earth and social justice. Both exile and diaspora could be understood as beckonings toward redemption, but a redemption not frozen in the shape of a highly centralized state. Instead, Jewish communities scattered everywhere could always strive toward redemption, never thinking they had or could fully accomplish redemption.

What is this "redemption"? I see it as the sacred process of moving toward a world of dignity for every human being and every species of our inter-breathing world. Dignity for humans in having enough food, shelter, healthcare, honorable work, spiritually fulfilling rest, participation in the music, arts, wisdoms of community, and equality with all others in making decisions about the future of a society we live in. Dignity for all species in living-space to thrive through patterns of rest from being constantly subjugated to human needs and desires.

The second hint of renewal was another book by two much younger authors: *For Such Times as These* by two Reconstructionist rabbis, Rabbi Ariana Katz and Rabbi Jessica Rosenberg. What I found in Katz-Rosenberg is a politically multidimensional view of what is emerging in many American Jewish activists: an alliance with other communities struggling to become fully part of an inclusive democracy—Blacks, immigrants, Indigenes, Latinos, women, LGBTQIA communities, perhaps Jews and Muslims and other religious minorities.

As a third important factor for hope, I was reenergized by the news that more than 100,000 Israelis were once again in the streets, demanding serious negotiations to make enough peace to bring the remaining hostages home alive. So far, there has been little application of the same emotions of love and compassion for suffering Palestinian civilians as for kidnapped Israeli civilians, but perhaps it will grow as the Spirit swells, breathes, and lights up the way forward. Or it may fade away as Israelis are overcome by traumas of their own and centuries past, by fear and by rage.

The fourth spark of get moving fire that renewed my energy was the commitment of thousands of American Jews to join others in demanding major changes in U.S. policy toward the two regimes that impose ultraviolence on the "other" of Abraham's peoples.

I felt as I read these books and the reports of a renewed Israeli and American Jewish uprising, a sense of a bedraggled Spirit rising from the depth of ocean to renew their breath. Creating prophetic diaspora communities that understand the value of knowing that we always live in exile. And seeking and winning more justice in society and Earth not to solidify it in repressive institutions. Each spring to sow seeds toward the next sprouts of justice and of peace. I was inspired by these books and actions because I could feel the Spirit rushing into my bloodstream, breathing into my life, a wind blowing into my world.

Fifth and finally, I learned from these present moments of renewed Jewish commitment to Jewish values to remember my long-ago encounter with the Spirit about diaspora. This came in the summer of 1969, when Israelis were still pondering what to do about very recently conquered Palestinian territories and the Palestinians who lived there. I remember a lunch that summer on the hills overlooking Jerusalem with Dan Leon, a self-critical kibbutznik who had written a book on the unrealized economic and political theory of the kibbutz. He was also one of the architects of a new Israeli political party, *Moked*. It was committed to peace with a new State of Palestine. I told him I was a Diasporanist. He said he had never heard of such a thing. We talked for hours about the futures of the Jewish people.

How could I so unexpectedly name myself a Diasporanist? I think because it was so clear that the Freedom Seder could only have been born in the United States, with its ongoing history of racism and the Black-led struggle for a fully inclusive democracy. I realize now that a prophetic diaspora Judaism is what I and three generations of Jews have been sowing seeds for. Of course, I am far from alone in the process of creating and living a prophetic diaspora Judaism. There have been—

- Rabbi Shefa Gold, who invented a whole new kind of prayer service based on chants of meaningful phrases from the tradition. She proclaimed "Love is at the center" for weekly study of the Song of Songs like a new book of Torah;
- Rabbi Jeff Roth, who co-founded (along with his partner Rabbi Joanna Katz) and directed Elat Chayyim, which for more than a dozen years brought together teachers, musicians, artists, to spread their wisdom, inspire creativity, and weave together amazing new holistic experiences; and then worked with and separately from Rabbi David Cooper and Shoshana Cooper in founding networks for teaching Jewish meditation;
- Jeffrey Dekro, who created Jewish money-centers to lend money to grassroots women's and

Black progressive businesses that could not attract investments from conventional sources, and then became a teacher of Zohar;
- Rabbi Marcia Prager, who shaped a unique rabbinical/cantorial/pastoral school for Jewish clergy without an expensive central residence;
- Rabbi Mordechai Liebling, who taught a series of pioneering courses at the RRC on the rabbi as activist for social change, and who brought Jewish wisdom and his own organizing skill to a multireligious, multiracial national network of progressive religious activists;
- Rabbi Brian Walt, who made his own Exodus from apartheid South Africa to join in founding first a pioneering progressive synagogue and then a rabbinic organization supporting human rights in the U.S. and in Israel/Palestine;
- Rabbi Jill Hammer and Holly Taya Shere, who co-founded the Kohenet Hebrew Priestess Institute to educate a new lineage of spiritual leaders based on the reexamination of ancient Hebrew-speaking women;
- Rabbi Shaya Isenberg, Bahira Sugarman, and Lynne Iser, who shaped a program to help aging Jews and others become elders able to transmit spiritual wisdom;
- Rabbi Tamara Cohen, who created in English a new Book of Lamentations for the wounded Temple Earth, and who wrote a series of feminist Passover Seders and new rituals for girls and women;
- Arlene Goldbard, who crystallized into action the idea of Rabbi Nate DeGroot to create new nonviolent versions of Chapter 9 of the Scroll

of Esther. This transformation of a sacred text pointed toward a new life for many sacred texts, especially those where women could express their own values, long silenced;
- Dr. Barbara Breitman, a psychotherapist, Rabbi Avruhm Addison, and Rabbi Zari Weiss, who drew from Hasidic practice and modern psychology to create the desire and the framework for spiritual direction as a Jewish practice and profession;
- Gerry Gorelick, who turned the previously bureaucratic job of executive director for a synagogue into a generous smoother of stony passages and taught the art to others.

Those are twelve clusters of people, a minyan-plus-two of those who have been creating a prophetic diaspora Judaism, mostly without naming their work "diaspora." I stop at a minyan-plus-two, because there is no real place to stop. Hundreds of American Jews have turned their attention to creating these projects because reality demanded it and the Spirit came to them as a wind to clear the way, or a fire to light the way forward.

In North America, the growth of a conscious prophetic diaspora Judaism would mean much more clear-headed commitment to the Spirit and opposition to the nationalism of white heterosexual, male, Christian political power.

Now, one final series of thoughts. I hope I leave as a legacy the making real of these elements, a deep rethinking and redoing of—

- Liturgy that starts from an ecological worldview, not a hierarchical one; Breath or Wellspring in referring to God, not Lord or King;
- Reimagination of Jewish festivals so that

"actifests" transform the future, not only celebrate or mourn the past;
- Selection of Prophets to be read/chanted in *haftarot* from outside the official list, our own generation and earlier;
- Creation of *tzedakah* collectives in which members give about two percent of their income to support Jewish and other campaigns for justice and shalom. These collectives and their tzedakah contributions would be governed by "one person, one vote" (not one dollar, one vote, as is the practice in present Jewish Federations);
- Reexamination of kashrut to include issues of human health, ethical treatment of animals and plants, ethical practices toward farm and restaurant workers, and support for regenerative agriculture;
- Reexamination of the roles of rabbis, cantors, and of other streams of Jewish knowledge, like the *kohenet* movement;
- Action and alliances toward a new economy more akin to the biblical cycle of practicing *shmita* (sabbatical-year rest) and *yovel* (fiftieth year redistribution) than to modern corporate industrialism.

Indeed, a new form of Judaism that struggles toward and fits into a just, democratic, and compassionate planetary society. The prophet Bob Dylan sang that "the answer is blowin' in the wind." The nature of the Spirit is to be the wind that history is blowin' in.

* * *

The Spirit has called me to adopt two new mottos for myself. One comes from Moses: the Spirit did not vanish from him as he learned he would die before he could continue leading the Godwrestling Folk on their next great task: settling in and on and with the promised soil. As he recalled that supernal Sinai—not when he stood there himself so many years before—he found himself saying that not only the whole people, even suckling babies, must have been present at that moment. The Spirit told him that even those not physically present had made themselves present in some unforgettable way. This meant Sinai would affect the world far into the future.

We stand in our generation in the same time-space: a crisis so deep that how we act can transform the future for a new world of sharing, love. and joy—or into a country and a planet of greed, selfishness, chaos, and death. The Spirit has turned itself into a question mark.

I had hoped the last U.S. presidential election would mean a great turning toward a world of love and justice for humans as well as more-than-human life. Instead, it means we face a world where much of human life, and more, is ruled by subjugation and killing. Hard to face, but necessary. All the more, another motto must be: those who are not yet physically present are in fact present—they are the future. We must work toward their becoming able to win elections on a series of immediate issues. And they must come together on something deeper than issues—Spirit. A Spirit of love rather than subjugation, killing, death. Our second motto comes from another old man, Rabbi Tarfon, being quoted by the Talmud: "I can't complete the Work that needs doing, but that doesn't mean I can quit."

So here's the beginning of not quitting: now we know that the entire evolutionary history of Earth and earthlings is a profound moral and ethical test. Is the human species able to learn love, empathy, and broader Community deeply enough to live well here and perhaps venture beyond this planet without endangering others? Or are we so addicted to power-over, greed, and exploitation that we will damage Earth and earthlings so lethally that we will be unable to sustain ourselves, let alone to venture forth and create friendship with whoever we meet?

Some of us define this great test as set for us by an external sacred force or being. Others define the test as arising intrinsically from ourselves, from our evolution and our history. Still others believe this is the level at which "religion" and "science" meet. For me, hearing YHWH well pronounced—a Breath—teaches me to celebrate the Interbreath of all life on this planet and perhaps beyond.

We ourselves have long been tugged by both impulses—to love and to subjugate. At last, we have created technologies to do each at a universal planetary level. Our impulse to subjugate has produced both nuclear weapons and the uncontrolled burning of fossil fuels. Either can wreck, kill, most life on Earth. We've also developed physical technologies that could feed, house, heal, and educate—"lead forth"—all humanity, as well as religious, spiritual, and ethical teachings and practices to make love for all life possible.

The killing technologies are quicker and easier to apply than the love practices. That present reality has been shaped by decisions of powerful people to invest more of their power in increasing their power to subjugate. And for me, I hear one whispered teaching from the Spirit: seeking to inspire, inform, and empower not only a new prophetic diaspora Judaism, but new ways of shaping spiritual courage with shared symbols and probably new symbols. To address these questions through transformational practices rooted in the wisdoms of each and every people. The present rush of power toward killing can be transformed toward loving, if other parts of our society will turn their hearts toward hearing the Spirit and turn their arms and legs and minds toward collective action. The urgent threat that increased subjugation will turn to massive killing means we have to choose love as quickly as we can.

So that is where my thinking takes me, to the brink of action. Beyond that brink, what comes next? I think first it is an effort to secure nonviolently what we have nonviolently won – conscious memory of the beginnings of trans-spiritual communities.

We have begun to create a Judaism, a Christianity, an Islam, a Hinduism, a Buddhism, many other "isms" with hundreds of thousands or millions of participants, and many local shamanic communities in which all humans can take a whole-hearted place in shaping the present and future of these spiritual communities—even the past, as we create new midrash on old wisdom in all our different sacred texts or practices. None of these have yet been transformed as a whole, but vital and creative parts of them have.

Varied communities have begun creating public rituals that transform our festivals into "actifests," transforming the future as well as celebrating or mourning the past. We might call for new prophets and new passages of their writings, arts, and music to communicate their wisdom in all our old and new ways to hear the Spirit: Martin Luther King, Jr., Rachel Carson, Abraham Joshua Heschel, Joanna Macy, Dorothee Solle, Richard Powers, Bayard Rustin, Judith Plaskow, Martin Buber, Edward Said, Gloria Steinem. We might need to do all this—and more—in secret, clandestine, subterranean ways depending on whether a fascist government tries to rub out those realities and memories, to invade our conversations.

Long ago, Moses called the Godwrestling People to choose between the blessing and the curse. He had specifics for each painted in huge letters on two mountains. Today we—not I, we—have the internet to reach each other and beyond. Feel free to share this message with your friends. I welcome your comments on this outline of theory and action.

Blessings to each of you and all of us as we face the crisis of democracy in America and Earth: blessings of truth, justice, and peaceful harmony. These, says the Talmud, are the three pillars of the world on which decent leadership must stand. But the Talmud also names three other pillars of the people if their leaders and rulers turn away from decency: wisdom from the past and beyond, prayer and meditation, acts of loving-kindness.

With the Spirit singing in my heart, I bless you-all with a world to come right here on Earth of all six pillars, three and three. And the seventh: time to rest, reflect, and love.

Afterword

Rabbi Phyllis Ocean Berman

Be careful if you tell a writer that you love his book; it may change your life!

For years in the 1970s and '80s, I made Passover Seders with up to thirty people. They were diverse as could be—teachers from the school I founded for intensively transmitting English to newly arrived immigrants and refugees; old friends; new friends who entered as friends of my children from their schools.

Some were families deeply learned in Judaism, some were Jews for whom seder was a brand-new adventure, some were not Jewish but spiritually hungry or adept in other communities. We had only one rule: no one could bring food unless they themselves were as strict as I about the special code of foods that were traditionally kosher for Passover.

In 1982, my guests included Lyn Fine and her nephew. She was one of the ESOL (English-to-Speakers-of-Other-Languages) teachers at my New York City school. She was Jewish-born and an active Buddhist in the lineage of Thich Nhat Hanh. Because she felt that bringing another person from her family to our seder demanded a real gift, and because I had forbidden food, she brought me a book as a gift.

When the two seders and *Pesach* ended, I opened the book, written by an author whose name I knew and whom I had seen in person but hadn't made any meaningful contact with. The book: *Seasons of*

Our Joy, a spiritual guide to and history of the Jewish festivals; the author: Arthur Waskow.

He began with a Hasidic tale: a man was on the road to go to study with his rebbe. Someone asked, "Are you going to study Torah with your rebbe?" "No," the hasid answered. "I'm going to study tying my shoelaces."

Arthur then dedicated the book to two men: Rabbi Max Ticktin and Rabbi Zalman Schachter-Shalomi. Both, he said, had taught him Torah and tying his shoelaces. I was dumbstruck. Max was my beloved Hillel rabbi from my years at the University of Wisconsin-Madison, where I studied as an undergraduate. Zalman was the *zeyde*/grandfather of the newly-emerging Jewish Renewal movement. He was energizing a post-Holocaust Judaism with a commitment to Earth, deep ecumenism, and feminist Judaism. He and Max were the two men whom I considered to be my spiritual forebears.

If Arthur had mentioned just one of them, I would have thought it was a coincidence. Instead, he'd chosen my two spiritual fathers. This man, I thought, must be a long-lost brother, and I sat down to read *Seasons* with the joy that I usually gave only to fiction.

I read the first chapter very slowly, focusing on every sentence and delighting in it as I would if it had been created by someone I was already lovingly close to. And at the end of that first chapter, I sat down and wrote Arthur a love letter.

Several months went by, and I heard nothing from him. In August, I went with my children to the second National Havurah Institute, an annual week-long gathering of adults and children to study, eat, pray, play, and become lifelong friends and family with one another.

In the mornings that week, I took a class with my son Josh and his friend Benjamin, and—as it turned out—with Arthur. At the end of the first class, I went up to Arthur and said, to his growing shock, "You're a fine teacher, and a great writer, but you're not a *mensch* worth a damn."

"Why are you saying that?" Arthur demanded. I told him that he hadn't answered my letter that I'd sent him in May. "Where did you send it?" he asked. Thinking that was a dopey question because he had placed his address in Washington, DC at the back of his book, I told him, "Where you said to in the book!"

"Oh," he said. "In May, I moved to Philadelphia and I have sacks of unopened mail in my basement. What did you write?"

And I've been telling him what I wrote ever since.

We are
Monkfish Book Publishing

...an independent press publishing spiritual and literary books from a diverse range of perspectives. Genres include memoirs, wisdom literature, fiction, and scholarly works of thought. Monkfish books appeal to the seasoned or novice seeker as well as to the general public looking for reliable sources on spirituality. The readers we had in mind when we began Monkfish in 2002 were devoted spiritual seekers, the type whose passion for the spiritual quest would lead them to read across a dazzling array of traditions: Buddhist, Hindu, Jewish, Christian, Muslim, Native American and more. It has always been our intent to publish works of spiritual authenticity for the general public as well as the specialist and scholar.

Our books are available from booksellers everywhere.

Use this QR code to see recently published books:

Use this one to sign-up for our monthly newsletter:

www.ingramcontent.com/pod-product-compliance
Lightning Source LLC
Jackson TN
JSHW032008231125
93802JS00001B/1